THE ARISTOCRACY
OF
SOUTHERN INDIA

THE ARISTOCRACY
OF
SOUTHERN INDIA

A VADIVELU

GYAN

Published by

Gyan Publishing House
5, Ansari Road
Daryaganj, New Delhi-110002
Phone: 011-47034999, 9811692060
E-mail: books@gyanbooks.com

Distribution Network
gyanbooks.com
India, USA, Canada, UK, Australia

ISBN: 978-93-6433-344-3 (PB)

First Published, 1903

2nd Impression 2025

Printed at: Gyan Press, Delhi.

THE ARISTOCRACY OF SOUTHERN INDIA
Author: A VADIVELU

THE ARISTOCRACY OF SOUTHERN INDIA

BY

A. VADIVELU,

Late Sub-Editor, "Evening Mail,"

Tutor of Oriental Languages to Civil and Military Officers,

Author of "Some Mysore Worthies,"

and

"Two Worthies of Southern India."

Madras:

PRINTED BY VEST AND CO., 11, MOUNT ROAD.

1903.

A LOYAL WELCOME GIFT

TO HIS ROYAL HIGHNESS

THE DUKE OF CONNAUGHT

IN MEMORY OF

HIS ROYAL HIGHNESS' VISIT

TO

INDIA

BY

A. VADIVELU.

A. VADIVELU.

TABLE OF CONTENTS.

H. H. The Nawab of Banganapally. C. S. I.

Kallikote Estate Press, Rambha.

HIS HIGHNESS THE NAWAB

SAIYID FATÊH ALI KHAN BAHADUR, C. S. I.,

OF BANGANAPALLI

(KURNOOL DISTRICT.)

Banganapalli, one of the Native States under the control of the Governor of Madras, is ruled by a Nawab whose claims to eminence are founded not upon any daring adventure or extraordinary learning, but upon the successful administration of his State, his steadfast loyalty to the British Crown, his increasing benificence to his subjects and his enlightened co-operation in movements for public good. Naturally noble-minded, his pursuits are just, his views are formed after mature reflection, and he is incapable of sentiments derogatory to the character of impartial and upright men. These exemplary qualities are just those which leave their lasting mark on the State, and entitle the ruler to the heartfelt gratitude and intelligent admiration of the people. There is no denying the fact that the State of Banganapalli has a very bright future before it, and it is with great pleasure that we give the first place in this series to a biography of His Highness the Nawab Saiyid Fatêh Ali Khan Bahadur C. S. I., the present ruler of Banganapalli.

The area of Banganapalli is about 275 square miles, and the population according to the Census of 1901, is 32,279. There are 13 Sub-Jaghirs in the State, and the annual income including them is a little more than 2½ lakhs of Rupees.

The Sub-Jaghirdars have no more powers within their own villages than taking measures to prevent the removal of the crops in cases of non-payment of kists, and then seeking the help of the Nawab for serving the defaulters with demand notices. They possess neither civil nor criminal powers. Suits arising within their jaghirs are exclusively triable by the Nawab's Courts, for the maintenance of which the Jaghirdars contribute.

In order to trace the history, from its origin, of the illlustrious family to which His Highness the Nawab belongs, it is necessary to go back more than three centuries, to the year 1051 (Hijri) or about 1633 A. D., when Sha Abbas II sat on the throne of Persia, assisted in Government by Saiyid Mahomed Khan Ruzvi, his Minister, who had two sons Saiyid Hussain Ali Khan, and Saiyid Thaher Ali Khan. On the death of this Minister, the Sha, who had been following with interest the progress made by Saiyid Thaher Ali Khan the younger son in education and culture, and appreciating his quick intelligence and comprehensive practical genius, conceived the idea of making him his Minister in preference to the elder, as a worthy successor to their father. When Saiyid Hussian Ali Khan, the elder son, heard this news, his rage knew no bounds and with determined spite, he commenced to plot against the life of Thaher Ali. But in all conspiracies where a number of persons have to be let into the secret, there is always the danger of some one of them proving a betrayer. So it was in this case. Somebody who knew the state of affairs informed their mother of the contemplated murder of her younger and better loved son. Thereupon, acting with a quickness of purpose and resolution rare among women, she lost no time in providing Thaher Ali with a well-filled purse, and informing him that his life was seriously in danger, succeeded in persuading him to leave the kingdom in secrecy and without the least delay.

About this time the Moghul Empire was at its zenith in wealth and power. The Moghul Emperor, who was a ruler of a very enlightened and liberal-minded type, had thrown open the high appointments of his State, both civil and military, to men of intelligence, culture, tact and integrity, irrespective of the place from which they might hail; and consequently all responsible appointments were at the time filled by the best educated men whom Persia could furnish.

Ali Adil Sha, who was then the ruler of Bijapur, in the Dekhan, and who had the intelligent co-operation of his Minister, Saiyid Asad Ali Khan, was a suzerain lord, and also a great patron of learning. On a certain evening, while the Minister was out in his palanquin, some Persians, who were among the retinue, on seeing a person in the coarse garb of a mendicant seated on a pial, left their lord, hastened to the pial, and paid their most respectful homage and reverence to the seemingly poverty-stricken personage seated there. As soon as the Minister reached home, he demanded from them, half in anger and half in surprise, an explanation regarding their strange behaviour and asked them to tell him what they knew about the dervish, whom they had run so eagerly to respect, leaving alone their own master. Then they told him that the man who was dressed like a dervish was the younger son of the late Minister of Persia, that for a long time he was given up for lost, nothing being known as to his fate, but that on that day they found him in the wretched plight that the Minister saw him in, and recognised him at once. Hearing this almost romantic story, Saiyid Asad Ali Khan sent one of them to fetch Thaher Ali, which was soon done. The coarse dress was removed and a rich dress suitable to his birth was at once put on. The respect due to a Minister's son was cheerfully accorded to him, while he himself showed that he fully deserved such esteem by his courtly manners, his witty conversation, his abundance of thought and his great eloquence. The Minister was delighted at his having found such a noble companion, and very desirous of cementing the connection more closely, allowed the friendship to rise to kinship by giving his daughter in marriage to Thaher Ali. Sometime after, Saiyid Asad Ali Khan died, and the ruler of Bijapur had to appoint a suitable successor. The former had sons, but his son-in-law, Thaher Ali, had had frequent occasions to impress the King with his nobility of behaviour, his uprightness and administrative capacity. The King naturally wished to confer the vacant ministership on Thaher Ali. This roused the malice and hatred of the sons of the deceased, and in their envy, they coolly shed the blood of their brother-in-law, attacking him in the night in a most cowardly manner. The Hindustani chronicler here characteristically adds that the heavens wore a gloomy countenance for sometime as if in keeping with the dark motives of the atrocious murderers, or as if in harmony with the darkness of the deed that was perpetrated on one, who, in life, shed light around him by his cheerful courtesy and kindliness of address. Poor Thaher Ali's wife, mad with grief at the murder of her husband, and exasperated by the cruel insults which her own brothers had heaped upon her, left the place at once with her two sons, Saiyid Asad Ali Khan and Saiyid Mahomed

Khan Nughdi, and found her way to a remote part of the world, Arcot, in Southern India, where she sought for, and obtained the bountiful help and powerful protection of the Nawab Sadut-ulla- Khan. The mind of Saiyid Ali was unhinged by the violent calamity that happened to his father, and his whereabouts were not known. The other, Saiyid Mahomed Khan Nughdi, was made a Munsubdar, and by dint of courage, resourcefulness and tact, he soon rose to be the Commander of a thousand horse in the service of the Nawab of Arcot. He subsequently married the grand daughter of the then Jaghirdar of Banganapalli, Fazlé Ali Khan, who was a descendant of the grand Vizier of Aurangazeb.

Banganapalli was originally under the sway of a chief named Raja Nanda Chakravarthi and his descendants. Ismail Adil Sha, the ruler of Bijapur, attacked and conquered, in 1643, Banganapalli and the surrounding Zamindaries, of which he gave Banganapalli as a Jaghir, in reward for services rendered, to his General, Siddu Simbul. At this time, Raja Gopal, the Zamindar of Kurnool, was a source of disturbance and annoyance to the surrounding Mahomedan Jaghirdars, and the King of Bijapur hearing of this, asked the Nawab of the Carnatic to proceed against Raja Gopal and subdue him. This was done, and in recognition of this useful service, Abdul Wahab Khan, the Nawab of the Carnatic, had the Kurnool Zamindari conferred on him. Later on, however, the whole of the Dekhan was conquered by Aurangazeb, and the Kingdoms of Golconda and Bijapur lost their independence and fell, and with these, Banganapalli and the surrounding Jaghirs passed directly under the sway of the Moghul Emperor, Aurangazeb. He appointed

Mahomed Bég Khan, a relation of his Minister, Mubaraz Khan, as Jaghirdar of Banganapalli, an appointment which was held by him in fealty till the dismemberment of the Moghul Empire. When, however, Asaf Jah (Nizam-ul-Mulk), the Viceroy of Hyderabad, assumed sovereign-power, Mahomed Bég Khan, declared his independence and constituted himself a petty Chieftain or Nawab. In the course of his southern tour, Asaf Jah recognised Mahomed Bêg Khan's title, and granted to him the territory in Jaghir. Mahomed Bêg Khan and his descendants held the Jaghir till 1758.

From the union of Saiyid Mahomed Khan Nughdi with the grand-daughter of Fazlê Ali Khan came two sons, Saiyid Hussain Ali Khan and Saiyid Asad Ali Khan. In 1150 Hijri, or about 1732 A.D., Gulam Ali Khan, a relation of Fazlê Ali Khan succeeded him as Jaghirdar of Banganapalli, and his sister-in-law was given in marriage to Saiyid Asad Ali. On the death of Ghulam Ali Khan, Saiyid Hussain Ali became Jaghirdar, and desirous of obtaining some military distinction, applied to Hyder Ali, then in the zenith of his power and glory, for an appointment under him, in the military service. For long, until the death of his patron Hyder, Hussain Ali Khan served in that capacity in Mysore, with benefit to the State and credit to himself. When Tippu succeeded, Hussain Ali who had become an invalid, took leave of his master and started for his native place, Banganapalli. But, unfortunately, he died on the way, and had not the pleasure of seeing again his native home. Tippu, on hearing of this sudden calamity, sent for the widow of Hussain Ali Khan and his children, who were four, named Saiyid Ghulam Ali Khan, Saiyid Fatêh Ali Khan, Saiyid Ahmed Ali

Khan and Saiyid Mustafa Ali Khan. But as the children were then of tender age and in poor health, the widow did not wish to subject them to the trying hardships which a long journey to Mysore would entail, and so delayed paying her respects to Tippu at his capital. This, the over-exacting and impulsive Tippu Sultan, construed into a deliberate slight, and instantly ordered the confiscation to the State, of the Jaghir of Banganapalli. A sense of her helpless position and misery struck her as if a keen shaft had pierced her brain, and her usual strength of mind and firmness under trial which had hitherto so often stood her in good stead now failed her, and in despair, she went away to Furrooknagar with her children. There, it so happened that on a certain day when Nizam Ali Khan, the then Nizam of Hyderabad, set out on a walk, he saw the four boys (her sons), who, though dressed so shabbily as to evidence their extreme destitution, deported themselves with much sober dignity falling in a line and making their obeisance to the sovereign in a manner which only the sons of noblemen learn as a part of their training. The Nizam who was struck by this inconsistency between their noble deportment and their needy appearance, called the boys to him, and asked them to tell him who they were. They related their melancholy history; on hearing which, the Nizam was moved with compassion for them, and directed them to appear the next day before the Minister, Musheer-ul-Mulk. They did so, and were told that they would be the recipients of an annual allowance of Rupees 3,000 each. Saiyid Hussain Ali Khan, their paternal uncle, who was in hiding at the time to escape the anger of Tippu against his family was sent for by the Nizam, and had much wealth and honor conferred upon him. Of the four sons of Asad Ali Khan mentioned above, the youngest, Mustafa, was distinguished for his manly behaviour and refined courtesy—qualities which among men of his nation are passports to eminence. The Minister considering him therefore a suitable husband for his grand-daughter made him his grand-son-in-law. Saiyid Ahmed Ali Khan, another of the brothers, married the daughter of a Munsubdar, and remained in Hyderabad for sometime. Saiyid Hussain Ali Khan, the uncle, by his talents and devotion to service won the esteem of the Nizam who conferred on him the title of Mazafar-ul-Mulk with a present of 800 sowars. At the head of this small army, he proceeded to Banganapalli accompanied by his nephews, attacked the place, and defeated the Sultan's army in the battle of Thammadapalli in 1205 (Hijri), or 1787 A. D., at which, one of his nephews, Saiyid Fatêh Ali was killed. When everything was over, Saiyid Hussain Ali Khan, celebrated the wedding of his daughter with Saiyid Ghulam Ali Khan, his eldest nephew, who was placed on the Musnud of Banganapalli as the rightful heir, though Hussain Ali Khan, the uncle, continued to reside at Banganapalli. Subsequently Ghulam Ali Khan remained for the most part of his time at Hyderabad, fought the battles of the Nizam, side by side with the English, against their common enemies, and distinguished himself for personal valour, on many a battle field. In recognition of these services, the Nizam conferred on him the title of *Mansurud-daulah Bahadur*. In a battle against the Maharattas, he lost the fingers of his right hand, and, as must happen among people who do most of their fighting with the sword, this put an end to his military career. Meanwhile, the uncle, Hussain Ali Khan, who was in Banganapalli, was suddenly taken ill, and on the news reaching Ghulam Ali Khan at Hyderabad, he left for Banganapalli, but before he reached the place, Hussain Ali Khan had died. Saiyid Ghulam Ali Khan had two sons and several daughters. He conferred the Jaghir of Banganapalli on his eldest son Saiyid Hussain Ali Khan, his second son Saiyid Fatêh Ali Khan being already in possession of a Jaghir in Hyderabad. Saiyid Ghulam Ali Khan died three years later in 1822 A. D. Hussain Ali Khan, having no male issue, adopted the younger son of Saiyid Fatêh Ali Khan, gave his daughter in marriage to him and made him heir-apparent. Saiyid Ghulam Ali Khan ascended the Musnud after the death of his uncle and father-in-law, Hussain Ali Khan. But Ghulam Ali Khan having died issueless, his elder brother Saiyid Asad Ali Khan's son Saiyid Fatêh Ali Khan, the present ruler of Banganapalli, ascended the Musnud.

In 1800, the Nizam transferred his control over Banganapalli to the British Government, when he ceded the Districts of Cuddappah and Bellary. In the Schedules attached to the Partition Treaty of Seringapatam, the territory of Banganaplli had been rated at 45,000 Canteroy Pagodas, or Rupees 1,31,250; but at the request of the Nizam who pleaded that the Jaghir had been granted for the maintenance of the numerous members of a noble family, the tribute was remitted by the British Government.

Mansurud-daulah, the Great, during his lifetime, with a view to prevent future disputes among his relations about property, made a settlement by which he assigned certain villages called sub-jaghirs to his cousins and the members of his family subject to the condition, that in the case of any one dying without heir, the sub-jaghir should revert to the ruling Nawab with the moveable and immoveable property of the deceased; and in cases of disloyalty among Sub-jaghirdars their property, both moveable and immoveable, should be confiscated, and the offenders deported beyond the limits of the State.

The family, however, was burdened with debt originally incurred chiefly by Saiyid Asad Ali Khan, brother of Munsurud-daalah, while he was Subadar of Cuddappah, and in consequence of embarrassments resulting from the Nawab Hussain Ali Khan's inability to satisfy his creditors, the Madras Government at the request of the Nawab himself undertook the management of the State from 1825, and after clearing the debt restored the Jaghir in 1848. Before the issue of the Sunnud of restoration Hussain Ali Khan died, leaving behind, as his adopted heir, his nephew Saiyid Gulam Ali Khan, who was also his son-in-law, having married his daughter Imdad Hussainee Begum. Both by matrimonial relationship and by right of descent, Saiyid Ghulam Ali Khan was recognised Jaghirdar by Government, and a Sunnud was issued to him in 1849, renewing the grant conferring civil and criminal jurisdiction unlimited, except in regard to capital punishments which alone require the special sanction of the Madras Government.

The following is the Sunnud :—

"Whereas the Right Honourable the Governor in Council of Fort Saint George was pleased, on the 12th July 1848, to confer upon Hoossain Ali Khan and his heirs for ever, in Jaghir, the lands of Banganapalli, free of peshcush and pecuniary demand; and whereas the said Hoossain Ali Khan has demised before the issue of a

Sunnud to confirm the same, and Ghulam Ali Khan has been recognised and acknowledged by the Government of Fort Saint George as his successor and representative: this Sunnud is granted to the said Ghulam Ali Khan as the present Jaghirdar.

The Jaghir of Banganapalli, conferred as aforesaid upon Hoossain Ali Khan and his heirs for ever free of peshcush and pecuniary demand, is hereby confirmed to you, Ghulam Ali Khan, as the representative of the said grantee Hoossain Ali Khan, now deceased.

You, therefore, shall have the general management of the revenue and police of your Jaghir, and also the duty of administering civil justice subject to the undermentioned conditions:—

You shall at all times maintain faith and allegiance to the Honourable Company; their enemies shall be your enemies, and their friends shall be your friends; you shall assist the Honourable Company to the utmost of your power against foreign and domestic foes; you shall maintain a strict watch over the public peace in your Jaghir; you shall not afford an asylum to offenders from the Company's Districts, but shall either deliver them up, or assist the Officer of the Company who may be sent in pursuit of them; you shall cause justice to be rendered to inhabitants of the Company's Districts and others who may have pecuniary claims on any of the inhabitants of Banganapalli.

In the administration of criminal justice within your Jaghir, you will abstain from the punishment of mutilating criminals, and will not sentence capitally, or execute persons capitally convicted, without the sanction of Government previously obtained; but will refer all cases appearing to you to call for such punishments, for the consideration and orders of the Governor in Council.

You shall be answerable to the Honourable Company for the good government of your Jaghir; and if ever it should happen that in consequence of misgovernment, the interposition of the Honourable Company should become necessary, the Governor in Council of Fort Saint George will, in such case, take such measures as may appear just and proper for restoring order, and providing for the security of the people.

On every occasion of your alienating any part of your lands, either rent free or on payment of favourable quit rent, you shall notify the particulars and conditions of such alienation to the Agent to the Governor of Fort Saint George, at Kurnool, or to any other officer who may from time to time be appointed by the Madras Government for the purpose, and you shall not confer any such inam lands, except under a written document, in which the terms and duration of the grant shall be distinctly specified, which duration is under no circumstances to extend beyond the enjoyments of the Jaghir by the grantee.

Given under the seal of the Honourable Company and signature of the Right Honourable the Governor in Council, in Fort Saint George, this twentieth day of March, one thousand eight hundred and forty-nine."

In 1862, the Jaghirdar received a Sunnud guaranteeing that the Government of India would permit any succession legitimate according to Moslim law, and it is as follows:—

"Her Majesty being desirous that the Government of the several Princes and Chiefs, who now govern their own territories, should be perpetuated, and that the representation and dignity of their Houses should be continued; in fulfilment of this desire, this Sunnud is given to you to convey to you the assurance that, on failure of natural heirs, the British Government will permit and confirm any succession to your State which may be legitimate according to Mahomedan Law.

Be assured that nothing shall disturb the engagement thus made to you, so long as your House is loyal to the Crown and faithful to the condition of the treaties, grants or engagements, which record its obligations to the British Government."

In 1861 Saiyid Ghulam Ali Khan Bahadur was made a Campanion of the Star of India. He died in 1868 without male issue, and succession to the Jaghir was contested by his widow, Imdad Hussainee Begum and his nephew and son-in-law Fatêh Ali Khan Bahadur, the present Nawab, whom the deceased had, during his life, nominated his heir.

His Highness the Nawab Saiyid Fatêh Ali Khan Bahadur, C.S.I., the son of Saiyid Asad Ali Khan Bahadur, the elder brother of Saiyid Ghulam Ali Khan Bahadur, C.S.I., the former Nawab of Banganapalli, was born at Banganapalli in 1848. Dissensions arising between the father and the uncle of the present Nawab, the family of Saiyid Asad Ali Khan Bahadur was compelled to leave the limits of the Jaghir, and betake itself to Hyderabad, by virtue of the Sunnud given by Mansurud-daulah, the founder of the State. The greater portion of the youth of the Nawab was spent in Hyderabad, though he and the other members of the family retained their hold on their sub-jaghir in Banganapalli. He was placed under the tuition of two competent Moulvis, who taught him Persian, Arabic and Hindustáni. Riding, shooting and instruction in other branches to suit the tastes and needs of a member of a highly respectable and ruling family, were not neglected. During the time he stayed at Hyderabad, he greatly distinguished himself by his intelligence, attainments, strong common sense and urbanity. A few years after, he married the daughter of his uncle Saiyid Ghulam Ali Khan Bahadur, but she was not destined to enjoy the pleasures of her wedded life long, the cruel hand of death snatching her away after three years. The Nawab then married a lady from the well-known family of Nurul-umra Bahadur of Hyderabad. By the first wife the Nawab has three sons, namely Saiyid Ghulam Ali Khan Bahadur, Saiyid Asad Ali Khan Bahadur, Saiyid Hussain Ali Khan Bahadur, and a daughter. When the news of the death of his uncle reached Hyderabad, the Nawab accompanied by his father arrived in Banganapalli. There was a strong contest for succession between Imdad Hussainee Begum, the *shadi-widow* of Saiyid Ghulam Ali Khan Bahadur; Nazimud-daulah, who was not related by blood to the late Jaghirdar, but was married to Shahar Bano Begum, his eldest nicka-daughter, and Saiyid Fatêh Ali Khan Bahadur, the present ruler. But the Government of India recognised the title of the third contestant in the following terms:—

1. "Nawab Ghulam Ali Khan, C.S.I., Jaghirdar of Banganapalli, having died on the 7th October 1868, it has become necessary for the Governor-in-Council to

determine who shall be declared to be the successor of the deceased Nawab in the Jaghir of Banganapalli.

2. From the correspondence above recorded, it appears that Ghulam Ali Khan died, leaving no direct lineal male heir, and that there are claimants to the Jaghir.

These are:—

1st. Imdad Hussainee Begum, shadi-widow of Ghulam Ali Khan, the recently deceased Jaghirdar, and shadi-daughter of Hussain Ali Khan, the predecessor in the Jaghir, and uncle of the said Ghulam Ali Khan.

2nd. Nazimood-daulah, who is not related by blood to the late Jaghirdar, but who is married to Shahar Bano Begum, his eldest nicka-daughter.

3rd. Fatêh Ali Khan, a son of Asad Ali Khan, elder brother of the late Jaghirdar. This claimant is married to Abasi Begum, the second nicka-daughter of the late Jaghirdar.

3. Imdad Hussainee Begum, the shadi-widow of the late Jaghirdar, claims on two grounds:—

1st. As nearest heir to her father Hussain Ali Khan, the predecessor in the Jaghir, and uncle of her late husband.

2nd. As co-partner in the Jaghir, which she pretends to have enjoyed in common with her late husband. The Government are unable to recognise as valid the grounds advanced by this claimant.

4. It is observed that the Sunnud of 1849 under which the late Jaghirdar held the State of Banganapalli, was not issued to Hussain Ali Khan, his immediate predecessor and his heirs, but to Ghulam Ali Khan himself and his heirs.

5. It is true that Imdad Hussainee Begum's father was put in possession of the Jaghir by an order of Government, dated 12th July 1848, that he would, except for his untimely death have in due course received a Sunnud confirming the Jaghir to him and his heirs, but such a sunnud was never actually issued and in deciding the present question of succession to the Jaghir, the Government must be guided by the Sunnud of 1849, which conferred the Jaghir on the late Ghulam Ali Khan and his heirs and in this document no allusion whatever is made to Imdad Hussainee Begum. On the other hand- her husband Ghulam Ali Khan, the nephew of the late Jaghirdar, is clearly recognised as the successor and representative of that dignitary.

6. When in 1849, the Government preferred Ghulam Ali Khan to his elder brother Asad Ali Khan, as successor to their uncle, the Jaghirdar, they were doubtless influenced by the consideration that Ghulam Ali Khan was son-in-law as well as nephew to the late Hussain Ali Khan. There were other cogent reasons for the selection in his relationship by blood to the last Jaghirdar, his experience in revenue matters and his favor with his father-in-law.

7. The Government are also unable to recognise the alleged co-partnery right with her late husband, and which is advanced by Imdad Hussainee Begum as furnishing a

ground for her claim to the succession. No such right is stated in the Sunnud of 1849, nor has it ever been recognised by Government.

8. For the reasons above adduced, the Governor-in-Council is of opinion that Imdad Hussainee Begum has failed to establish any claim to succeed to the Jaghir.

9. The second claimant to the Jaghir, Nazimood-daulah who married Shahar Bano Begum, the eldest nicka-daughter of the late Jaghirdar Ghulam Ali Khan, is not by blood related to the late Jaghirdar. His claim rests solely on a document executed jointly by the late Jaghirdar and his wife Imdad Hussainee Begum at the time of the claimant's marriage with the late Jaghirdar's nicka-daughter in 1863, by which the Jaghirdar engaged to make Nazimood-daulah his heir in the Jaghir, in case he should die without male issue, and solemnly declared that he would make no other settlement of the Jaghir to the prejudice of this engagement.

10. The Government are unable to recognise this document as being of any effect in supporting Nizamood-daulah's claim. Such a deed is, in their opinion, null and void.

1st. Because it never received the assent of Government.

2nd. Because it contemplated a departure from the sense of the Sunnud of 1849, by which the Jaghir was secured to the heirs of Ghulam Ali Khan.

Under these circumstances the claims of Nazimood-daulah is inadmissible.

11. The third applicant for the Jaghir of Banganapalli is Fatêh Ali Khan, eldest son of Saiyid Asad Ali Khan, the elder brother of the late Jaghirdar, Ghulam Ali Khan. He is married to a nicka-daughter of the late Jaghirdar.

12. The Governor-in-Council is of opinion that this claimant is, after his father Asad Ali Khan who advances no claim to the succession, the nearest heir in the sense of the Sunnud of 1849 to the deceased Jaghirdar Ghulam Ali Khan.

In addition to his near relationship by blood, and his connection by marriage, Fatêh Ali Khan was designated by the late Jaghirdar as his successor in a deed executed on the 22nd June 1866, in the presence of the Collector of the Kurnool District.

Although this deed is of no effect without the confirmation of the Government, it was formally communicated to the Civil Officer representing the Government, as expressive of the selection of a successor made by the late Jaghirdar, and in conformity with the intention of the Sunnud of 1849.

13. After a careful consideration of the claims above described, His Excellency the Governor-in-Council resolves to direct the issue of a Sunnud conferring on Fatêh Ali Khan and his heirs for ever, in Jaghir, the lands of Banganapalli free of peshcush and pecuniary demand in the same conditions as those contained in the Sunnud of 1849.

14. From the letter received from the Collector of Kurnool, dated 7th January, it appears that under the arrangements made by the late Jaghirdar Ghulam Ali Khan, in which arrangements, Fatêh Ali Khan concurs, provision has been made for the late Jaghirdar's family.

15. The Collector of Kurnool is directed to communicate this order to Fatêh Ali Khan, to Imdad Hussainee Begum, and Nazimood-daulah."

That a member of the illustrious family of the Banganapalli Nawabs should by right of descent assume the rulership of the State was in itself a very popular event. It was an augury of prosperity to the subjects of Banganapalli. Personally the Nawab had inspired the people of the place with love, admiration and esteem for him. He was proclaimed Nawab with the usual solemnities. Mr. Chase, the then Collector of the Kurnool District, installed him on the *guddi* of his ancestors, offering him his sincerest congratulations and wishing him many years of health, prosperity, and usefulness in the position to which he had succeeded.

Three years after the above Sunnud was issued the widow of the late Nawab again commenced to annoy the present ruler by defying his authority. The Collector of the District proposed to constitute a punchayet to consider the dispute and bring about a reconciliation between the present ruler and the widowed Begum. The subject came up for consideration before the Government of Madras when the following proceedings were passed :—

"The Government observe that subject to the sovereign authority of the British Gevernment, the Nawab of Banganapalli possesses under Sunnud limited criminal jurisdiction in his Jaghir, but has the uncontrolled administration of civil justice, and of revenue matters, and is answerable for the good government of the Jaghir. There are certain obligations imposed upon him in regard to his general management, but nothing which in any way whatever invests the Collector of Kurnool with any appellate authority or requires the interference of Government, except in cases of misgovernment.

2. In the present instance it is evident that ill feeling on the part of the widow of the late Nawab who claims the succession is inducing her to set the Nawab in defiance, but she must be given to understand that his authority must be respected and the Government cannot sanction any proceeding which would have the appearance of weakening that authority.

3. On these principles the Government cannot approve Mr. Chase's proposal to constitute a punchayat, presided over by a Government officer to determine the disputes between the Nawab and the widowed Begum, and would be unable to sanction any such arrangement. They regret that Mr. Chase should have taken the step of suggesting it to the Nawab and the opposite parties without previous reference to Government.

4. They desire that Mr. Chase will take an early opportunity of visiting Banganapalli and impressing on the Begum kindly but firmly that she must accept the present state of things, and refrain from defying the Nawab's authority, but that if she persists in her present line of conduct, it may be necessary to arrange for her residing beyond the limits of the Jaghir at either Kurnool or Hyderabad.

5. Mr. Chase will also inform the Nawab that his authority in the matter will be supported by Government so long as he behaves with justice and consideration to the Begum."

The first wife of the Nawab was a highly talented lady; she was conversant with Persian, Arabic and

Hindustani. She took an active interest in female education. Her noble disposition, her generous instincts, her dislike of ostentation, her respect of all that is true and good, were some of the characteristics calculated to raise her in the estimation of those who had known her personally and render her an object of admiration, gratitude and love to her dependants. In 1886 she obtained the Nawab's permission to visit Palestine. She, accompanied by her children, went on a pilgrimage to Karbala and other holy places. The Nawab being anxious about the safety of his family sought the assistance of Government, through the Political Agent, when they issued the following general letter :—

Letter————

TO ALL BRITISH AUTHORITIES WHOM IT MAY CONCERN.

"The bearer, who is the Begum of the Nawab of Banganapalli, a native State, within the jurisdiction of the Government of Madras, is proceeding with her children and suite, consisting of about 30 followers, on a pilgrimage to Ninevah (Karbala in Irak Arabi), and expects to pass through Basurah, Bagdad, Najef, Samrah, and Kazmeen. It is requested that the Begum may be treated with due respect, and that such help may be afforded to her, both on her forward and return journey, as she may be in need of "

It is hardly necessary for us to say that the Begum was treated with due respect and attention in her travels, and while at Bagdad an escort of eight sowars was furnished to her by the Turkish Governor of that place. She died one year after her return from Karbala.

There are different grades of reception accorded to Native Princes within the jurisdiction of a Governor. In order that we may give a full idea of the Nawab's position as the Ruler of a State, we give below the ceremonies obeserved when he visited, and was visited by, H. E. the Governor of Madras, and H. E. the Viceroy and Governor-General of India :—

RECEPTION BY HIS EXCELLENCY THE GOVERNOR OF MADRAS, OF THE NAWAB OF BANGANAPALLI.

"At 4-45 P.M., on Thursday, the 30th December, 1895, H. E. the Governor received a visit from the Nawab of Banganapalli, at Government House, Madras.

The Under-Secretary to Government in the Departments under the Chief Secretary and an Aid-de-Camp, to His Excellency proceeded in one of the Governor's carriages from Government House, at 4-10 P.M., for the purpose of escorting the Nawab, from Moore's Gardens.

The deputation was received at the Nawab's house, by his eldest son. The Nawab and the deputation then drove to Government House in the Governor's carriage, the Nawab's eldest son, and an Officer of the Nawab's Staff following in one of the Nawab's carriages.

On alighting from the crriage, the Nawab was met by the Military Secretary to His Excellency the Governor, who, with the deputation led him up the stairs. The Nawab was received at the top of the stairs by the Private Secretary to His Excellency, who conducted him to the Reception room.

The Governor received the Nawab seated, and showed him to a seat at his right hand.

On the right of the Nawab was seated the Under-Secretary, the Private and Military Secretaries to the Governor, and His Excellency's personal staff.

After a short conversation the Nawab's attendants were introduced by the Aid-de-camp.

At the close of the interview, attar and pan were given by the Governor to the Nawab, and by the Under-Secretary to the Nawab's attendants.

The ceremonies at the Nawab's departure were same as those observed at his arrival.

The Nawab was escorted to and from Government House by a party of the Body Guard, consisting of one Non-commissioned Officer, and eight sowars.

The Entrance Hall of Government House was lined by an armed party of the Body Guard (twelve).

A Native Officer's mounted party (sixteen) of the Body Guard with a trumpeter proceeded in front of the grand entrance and also the House-guard of Native Infantry; these together saluted on the arrival and departure of the Nawab.

RETURN VISIT OF H. E. THE GOVERNOR OF MADRAS, TO THE NAWAB OF BANGANAPALLI.

His Excellency the Governor returned the visit of the Nawab of Banganapalli, on Wednesday, the 4th December, at 4-45 P.M.

A deputation consisting of the Nawab's eldest son, and an officer of the Nawab's Staff waited on the Governor, at Government House, at 4-30 P.M. H. E. the Governor started under a salute of seventeen guns, and was attended by the Under-Secretary in the Departments under the Chief Secretary, and two Aides-de-camp.

The Nawab received the Governor at the step of the carriage at the Nawab's residence, and conducted him to a seat at his right hand.

On the right of the Governor sat the Under-Secretary, and the Aid-de-camp. On the left of the Nawab sat his attendants.

After a short conversation, the Nawab's attendants were received by him.

At the close of the interview, attar and pan were presented by the Nawab to the Governor, and by the Nawab's principal attendants to the British Officers present.

The ceremonies which attended the Governor's arrival were repeated at His Excellency's departure.

A guard of honor was drawn up at the Nawab's residence, and saluted the Governor on his arrival and departure.

RECEPTION BY HIS EXCELLENCY THE VICEROY AT MADRAS, OF THE NAWAB OF BANGANAPALLI.

At 12-15 p.m., on Friday, the 25th November, 1892, His Excellency the Viceroy and Governor-General, received a visit from the Nawab of Banganapalli, at Government House, Madras.

The Political Officer on duty with the Nawab, accompanied him to Government House.

On alighting from his carriage, the Nawab was met by an Aid-de-camp to the Viceroy, and was received at the top of the stairs by the Officer on Special duty in the Foreign Department, who conducted him to His Excellency's presence.

The Viceroy received the Nawab seated, and motioned him to a seat at his right hand.

On the right of the Nawab was seated the Political Officer, and beyond him such of the Chief's attendants, not exceeding two in number, as are entitled to a seat in Durbar.

On the left of the Viceroy were seated the Officer on Special duty in the Foreign Department, and His Excellency's personal staff.

After taking his seat, the Nawab rose and presented a nazar of 31 gold mohurs, which were touched and remitted.

After a short conversation, the Nawab's attendants were introduced by the Political Officer, and offered nazars of one gold mohur each, which were also touched and remitted.

At the close of the interview, attar and pan were given by the Viceroy to the Nawab, and by the Officer on Special duty in the Foreign Department to his attendants.

THE CEREMONIES AT THE NAWAB'S DEPARTURE WERE THE SAME AS THOSE OBSERVED AT HIS ARRIVAL.

When H. R. H. the then Prince of Wales, now King Edward VII, visited Madras, the Nawab was one of those introduced to His Royal Highness, at the Government House. After a short conversation with the

Nawab, His Royal Highness presented him with a silver medal, and a double-barrelled revolver of excellent workmanship.

The following Sunnud, dated Fort William, 24th January 1876, signed by His Excellency Lord Northbrook, the then Viceroy, was given to the Nawab, conferring upon him as a hereditary distinction the title of *Nawab* :—

"In recognition of your position as the Jaghirdar of Banganapalli, I hereby confer upon you the title of *Nawab* as a hereditary distinction to be assumed by your successors on formal recognition of their succession."

On the occasion of the Golden Jubilee of Her Majesty the late Empress of India, the Political Agent for Banganapalli, communicated the following to the Nawab with compliments and best wishes for his long life, wealth and prosperity :—

"YOUR HIGHNESS,

On the auspicious occasion of the celebration of the Jubilee of Her Majesty the Queen, Empress of India, I address Your Highness, whose loyalty to the British Throne and Government is unquestioned, with the desire of associating you with the expression of joyfulness at this event, which is general throughout India, and of conveying to you an expression of my high consideration, and of my best wishes for the continued prosperity of Your Highness, and of Your Highness's State."

The Jubilee was celebrated in Banganapalli with the greatest enthusiasm. All the buildings in the Town of Banganapalli having been previously whitewashed, the festivities commenced by a banquet given by the Nawab Syed Fatêh Ali Khan Bahadur, C.S.I., to the

Mohammedan population, which lasted until 2-30 P.M. At 3 P.M., the Nawab held a Durbar, which was attended by all the nobles of the Court, and the representatives of the agricultural community. At 5-30, a congratulatory address was read in English and Hindustani, and received with cordial cheers. This was followed by prayers in the Durbar Hall for the long life and prosperity of Her Majesty, the Queen Empress. After this, followed the release of eight prisoners from the State Jail, and a reduction in the sentences of four others. This was succeeded by a salute of 31 guns from the ramparts of the Fort, and a distribution of attar and betel. From 6 p.m., till the dawn of the following day, the palace, public buildings, and the houses generally were illuminated with coloured and plain lights, whilst fireworks, music, and dancing continued during the night. On the morning of the 17th, a distribution of food was made to about 8,000 persons, including visitors to the festival from the outlying districts; and at night a similar feasting took place, and there was another display of fireworks. During both the celebration days, prayers were offered in the temples and mosques for Her Majesty's long life and prosperity, and a distribution of alms was made to the poor. The Nawab defrayed all the charges.

The Nawab was made a Member of the Central Committee of the Imperial Institute in 1887, when the following correspondence took place between the Chief Secretary to the Government of Madras, and the Nawab:—

"SIR,

I am directed to inform you that, since the receipt of your letter expressing willingness to serve on the Central Committee of the Imperial Institute, and to subscribe towards that institution, a telegram has been received from the Government of India to the effect that the subscription qualifying for membership of the Committee will, in ordinary cases, be Rs. 500 and upwards; but as you have been specially selected by His Excellency the Governor in Council on the ground of your general qualifications, I am to state that there will be no objection on your part to subscribe the above amount. The Government, would, however, like to be informed of the sum you propose to subscribe."

"DEAR SIR,

With great pleasure I acknowledge the receipt of your letter No. 1132, dated 12-8-87, and state that I feel fully sensible of the high honor conferred on me by His Excellency the Governor in Council in adding my name to the list of subscribers to the Imperial Institute, which honor I gratefully acknowledge. I beg to express my regret that my limited means do not permit me to subscribe to the noble and laudable object which the Institute represents, more than the very limited sum of Rs. 4,000. I request you will kindly try to make this acceptable to the Government of India conveying, at the same time, my heart-felt thanks for the very benevolent intentions cherished by Her Imperial Majesty towards her loyal Indian subjects."

When the news of the death of the Queen was received at Banganapalli, the Nawab ordered the closing of all Public Offices at once, and mourning was observed for eight days. Prayers were offered in all mosques and temples. The Nawab sent a message of condolence, through the Potitical Agent to the Governor of Madras, to be communicated to the bereaved members of the Royal Family.

It will not be out of place if we should give here some of the most important reforms effected by the Nawab in the interests of his subjects.

Formerly there was only one Amildar under the immediate directions of the Jaghirdar (as he was then known). All the civil and criminal cases would be taken before him and he would hear and dispose of them, without any particular procedure, the Amildar helping him as an interpreter. The Nawab has now introduced a new system by which the State is administrated on modern principles. A Tahsildar, assisted by a suitable establishment, is appointed. He is in charge of the State Treasury under the direct supervision of the Nawab. The Tahsildar is responsible for the due collection of revenue, and also for the settlement of boundary disputes, and other cases connected with land tenure. There is a Magistrate exclusively entrusted with criminal powers. The Munsiff is empowered to decide civil suits involving a sum up to Rupees 3,000. The Sadar Court presided over by the Nawab is the final appellate authority over the decisions of the above said courts. Besides being the Appellate Court, the Sadar Court exercises original civil and criminal jurisdiction: in civil suits of above Rupees 3,000 and in grave criminal offences. The law in vogue in the British territory is observed here.

The Jail building is a new one on improved sanitary principles. There is a Eurasian in charge of it, and the local Medical officer is the ex-officio Superintendent.

There is also a garden attached to the Jail for the prisoners to work in.

The State has now a well-trained Police force under the able supervision of a Police Inspector, who had had good experience in the Madras Police Force. There are also three out-stations for the convenience and the safeguarding of the villages belonging to the State.

The State dispensary is worked on English lines under a well-experienced and diplomæd Medical Officer of the Civil Medical Department, Madras. The hospital is resorted to not only by the inhabitants of the capital, but also by those living in the surrounding British tracts. The Medical Officer has a competent assistant, besides three compounders. It is satisfactory to observe that a diplomæd midwife is also employed on the staff of the dispensary. The supply of medicine is quite ample, and the instruments are kept in very good order.

There are schools for boys in the head quarters and also in the principal villages. At head quarters there is an English school which teaches up to the Primary Standard.

In October 1873, Saiyid Ghulam Ali Khan Bahadur, the heir-apparent was born. When the news of his birth was announced, it was received with pleasure and delight everywhere, and the people were very jubilant over the event. Proper arrangements were made for the Prince's education, and the services of a suitable tutor were secured to teach him English, Hindustani, Persian and other subjects. He has grown to be an intrepid rider, and a capital huntsman, and bears a very good character. He married the daughter of his uncle, Saiyid Murtuza Ali Khan Bahadur, on the 7th December, 1900. He has a taste

H. H. THE FIRST PRINCE OF BANGANAPALLY.
H. H. THE THIRD PRINCE OF BANGANAPALLY.
H. H. THE SECOND PRINCE OF BANGANAPALLY.

Kallikotestate Press, Rambha.

for history, and has a large collection of historical and biographical works both in English and Urdu.

The second Prince, Saiyid Asad Ali Khan Bahadur, is a great reader. He has a large collection of standard works, and his taste for English literature has been growing from day to day. His wife, whom he married seven years ago, comes from the well-known family of Nurul-umra Bahadur of Hyderabad. The third Prince, Saiyid Hussain Ali Khan Bahadur is very intelligent and painstaking in the acquirement of knowledge.

The Nawab must be proud of his sons. They are all noble, generous, and gentlemanly, and they pay particular attention to the fact that their household ought to be sober and well-governed. They do not love show, but everything from their dress to their equipage, is simple and nice. Such are their distinguishing traits, and these amiable features leave their impress upon all who come in contact with them.

As soon as the Nawab was installed on the *Guddi*, he found out, as most essential things to peace and good government, the instilling into public officers an adequate sense of their responsibility, and a diligent enquiry into and an early redress of all grievances and abuses. To establish his reputation as a just and enlightened ruler, the Nawab has had to study carefully the important changes in public opinion, and to found his judgment on public affairs on a minute and elaborate consideration of the arguments for and against. He is sincerely religious-minded and God-fearing, and in matters, great or small, he never allows any prejudices to warp his judgment, and in all circumstances keeps his temper equable and unruffled. He is a devout believer in the teachings of Mahomed the Prophet, and profoundly learned in the Koran. To understand the truths mentioned in it, he is of opinion, that one needs not a capacious intellect, a disciplined mind or a great store of what the world calls learning, but a heart so humbled by the spirit of God as to receive them as His Testimony in "the love of the truth." Suffice it to say that as an administrator, he exercises a decided influence for good upon his subjects, and that he is held in the highest estimation by people in and around Banganapalli, for his sterling character, impartial justice, and rigid honesty of purpose. All these qualities claim a due recognition at the hands of Government and a Knighthood from the Government of India, all right-thinking people must grant, will prove but a deserved reward. From what has been said of the Nawab, it is evident that he will always retain the confidence of the paramount power, and be the protector of the rights, privileges, and liberties of his subjects, who form the backbone and sinews of his State; and his sincere convictions and sound practical applications of them are of such value that it is impossible to over-estimate their worth. As constancy of conduct and fixity of principle are the characteristics of the Nawab, characteristics which claim their attention by their very rarity, they are sure to impress any student of the history of our times with a feeling of high esteem for the illustrious personage in whom such virtues are united.

H. H. The Maharajah of Bobbili. K. C. I. E.

Kallikote Estate Press, Rambha

H. H. THE MAHARAJAH OF BOBBILI

(*VIZAGAPATAM DISTRICT*).

The Maharajah of Bobbili was the only prince of Southern India, on whom the title of "Maharajah" was conferred by the Government of India, in the last year of the nineteenth century during the life-time of Her Majesty the late Empress of India. He is one of those distinguished noblemen whose services have greatly contributed to widen the influence and support the renown of the paramount power.

The Bobbili Zemindari is one of the most ancient Zemindaries in India. It is included in the Vizagapatam District, Madras Presidency, and possesses a very interesting history. It is situated in lat. 18°22′ to 18°46′ N., long. 83°10′ E., is surrounded by the British taluks of Chipurupalli, Gajapatinagaram, Salur, Parvatipur, Palconda and Chicacole, and consists of the Pergunnahs (Tanas) of Bobbili, Rajam, Kavitey and Sitanagaram, each of which is under the charge of an officer called Ameen. The Zemindari, together with the proprietary estates eventually bought, is about 920 sq. miles in area, and contains 202 Jeroyiti villages, 70 agraharams and 6 mokhasas. Its revenue is about 5 lakhs of rupees, including the value of about 3,567 garces of paddy, which is paid in kind. The peishcush is Rs. 95,315 and the land-cess, Rs. 32,467.

There are 14 indigo factories in the Zemindari; most of them are leased to Messrs. Arbuthnut and Co.

The chief town is Bobbili, the residence of the Maharajah. (Lat. 18°34′ N., long. 18°25′ E.) It is about 70 miles north-west of Vizagapatam. Sir M. E. Grant Duff, who visited Bobbili in 1883, describes it as "a clean and well-kept town, furnished with all the appliances of Anglo-Indian civilisation—schools, hospitals and what not —all within a walk of the remains of the Old Fort, where 126 years ago was enacted one of the most ghastly stories which even Indian History has to record."

The Bobbili family belongs to the tribe known as Velama Doras, who (according to Orme) "esteem themselves the highest blood of Native Indians next to the Brahmins, equal to the Rajputs, and support this pre-eminence by the haughtiest observances, insomuch that the breath of a different religion, and even of the meaner Indians, requires ablution." The men of this race are, as a rule, well-built and of a warlike disposition.

The founder of the house of Bobbili was the fifteenth in descent from the founder of the house of Venkatagiri, from which eminent family sprang the present ruler of Bobbili. In 1652, Sher Mahomed Khan, the Nawab of Chicacole, on behalf of the Moghul Emperor, marched against Vizagapatam, when the former was accompanied by two chiefs, *viz.*, Nirvana Rayappa, generally known as Pedda Rayadu, the fifteenth Rajah of Venkatagiri, and Madhava Varma, the ancestor of the Vizianagaram family. In recognition of the meritorious services rendered to the Nawab by the former chief, the Moghul Emperor conferred upon him the grant of the Rajam Estate, where the chief built a fort and in token of his gratitude towards the worthy donor named it Bebbocly (the royal tiger), in honor of his patron's designation, Sher (tiger). From Bebbooly the name of the town and Zemindari has been corrupted into Bobbili. In addition to the grant of this valuable estate, the further recognition of the chief's services by the Moghul Emperor was the conferring of the titles of Rajah and Bahadur, and also the right to use a white flag, dhanka, nowbat and other insignia of royalty. After establishing every thing on a firm basis, Rajah Pedda Rayadu Bahadur Garu returned to his place, nominating his son Lingappa as the ruler of the newly obtained Raj. Rajah Lingappa Bahadur, who had inherited the valour and prowess of his father was also very serviceable to the Moghul Emperor whenever there was any disturbance. A son of the General Sher Mahomed Khan went on a hunting excursion on a certain day, when he was surprised, captured and kept in confinement by a Fattooridar at Rangavaka near Palasa in the Ganjam District. The General's request to the Rajah Lingappa Bahadur to rescue his son met with a favourable response, and the result was, that the Fattooridar was taken prisoner and the boy brought out of confinement. The solicitude, intrepidity, and the most opportune help of the Rajah Bahadur so much won the favor and esteem of the General, that he commended him to the favorable notice of the Moghul Emperor, whose admiration of the promptitude and generous nature evinced by the Rajah became so great, that he ordered the free enjoyment of as many villages in his State as he could in one night adorn with festoons. This was accordingly done, and the Rajah became the lord of twelve villages. The Moghul Emperor went a step further, and conferred the title of Ranga Row (Lord Ranga Vaka-Vaka, meaning a seat or resort of a Fattooridar, otherwise meaning victor in battle). This title has since been used by all succeeding members of the Bobbili family.

The sixth of the Rajahs whose reign is memorable on account of the Battle of Bobbili, was Rajah Gopala Krishna Ranga Row Bahadur Garu. In 1756 the disorderly behaviour of the Poligars called for measures of repression, and M. Bussy marched with a European force to restore order. On his arrival in Vizianagram, he was assured by the Rajah that the Chief of Bobbili was the instigator of all disturbances. We take the following from the Madras Manual of the Administration by Dr. Macleane, about the attack on the Fort of Bobbili, and its result :—

"The Rajah of Vizianagram to testify his own loyalty joined the French with a force of 11,000 men to assist in crushing his rival. Before attacking the latter, M. Bussy offered the chief a pardon for the past, and land of equal value elsewhere, if he would abandon his ancestral estate, but the offer was refused. The attack on the fort of Bobbili is one of the most memorable in Indian History. At daybreak, the field pieces began to play on the mud defences, practicable breaches were at once made, and the assault sounded. After four hours' desperate fighting, hand to hand, Bussy called off his men to allow the cannon to widen the breaches. A second assault was then ordered, but with no better results; for not a man had gained footing within the ramparts when five hours later Bussy again withdrew the storming party to repeat the argument of artillery. The defenders now recognised their desperate position, and collecting their wives and families put them to death, and returned to their posts. The assault soon recommenced; and when at sunset,

Bussy entered the fort as victor with the remnant of his army, it was only because every man of the garrison was dead or desperately wounded. An old man, however, crept from a hut, and leading a child to Bussy presented him as the son of the dead chief. Four other men had preserved their lives, and two nights later when the Vizianagram camp was buried in sleep, they crept into the Rajah's tent, and before the sentries discovered and shot down the assassins, they had stabbed the Rajah to death with thirty-two wounds. The child, Chinna Ranga Row, saved from the slaughter, was invested by Bussy with the chiefship of the lands that had been offered to his fathers."

The Chief, whose reign was longer than that of any of his predecessors, was Rajah Sweta Chalapati Ranga Row Bahadur who became famous far and wide on account of his munificent gifts. During his reign every charitable undertaking in the District found in him a ready, willing and benevolent patron. In 1832 serious disturbances broke out in the Ganjam and Vizagapatam Districts. The Rajah devised all means in his power and succeeded in apprehending Kambara Venkatarayadu and other Fattooridars who were the cause of the disturbance and delivered them to Mr. Russell, the Special Commissioner, who was appointed by the Government of Madras. It is to the credit of the same Rajah that he made large additions to the estate.

The Rajah who had no issue adopted one of the sons of the Rajah of Pittapur as his heir and successor, and died on the 18th August 1862.

Rajah Sitarama Ranga Row Bahadur, the adopted son of the deceased Rajah, ruled only for five years. He gave a marked impetus to the promotion of education, and it was he who started the Anglo-Vernacular School at Bobbili in 1864. It is to be greatly regretted that he died at the comparatively early age of 23 years.

Rani Lakshmi Chellayamma Garu succeeded her deceased husband. Though the lady was very young when the onerous duty of guiding the destiny of a large State devolved on her, yet her enlightened policy, her liberal-heartedness and her statesmanship enabled her to excel most of her contemporaries. She very prudently appointed a Dewan of well-tried abilities, who had already given proof of his uprightness and energy during the reign of her late father-in-law. Her liberality during the great famine in Bengal, in 1873, is still a household word in many places. She sent paddy of the value of Rupees 50,000, and this noble conduct met with the approbation of the Government of India, which recorded its high sense of appreciation of the generosity of the Rani. She was represented by her Dewan, when H. R. H. the Prince of Wales, now our Most Gracious Emperor, King Edward VII, visited Madras, and had the special honour of receiving a medal from His Royal Highness. In February 1876, the Government of India, in token of their appreciation of the wisdom displayed by this lady, conferred on her the title of "Rani" as a personal recognition. A rebellion broke out at Bastar, when the Rani, with her usual promptitude, rendered her share of help in quelling it. We avail ourselves of this opportunity of giving publicity to the following letters about the Rani, who died on the 7th May 1887 :—

"MADAM,

I am directed by the Government to communicate to you, their thanks for the assistance you rendered to them, in the march of an army for the crushing of the rebellion, that recently broke out in Bastar, and for other convenient arrangements that you made for them in that connection. I have, therefore, gladly communicated the matter to you and enclosed an extract from the order.

(Signed) * * *

Acting Agent to the Governor."

OFFICE OF GOVERNOR'S
AGENT,
22nd July, 1876.

EXTRACT FROM THE PROCEEDINGS OF THE MADRAS GOVERNMENT, JUDICIAL DEPARTMENT, 26TH JUNE 1876, NO. 1279.

* * * *

"Mr. Goodrich will also convey to His Highness the Maharajah of Vizianagaram and to the Rani of Bobbili the thanks of Government for the assistance and facilities they afforded to the movements of the troops on the late occasion.

(True Extract).

(Signed) * *

Acting Agent to the Governor."

COPY OF A LETTER FROM MR. GARSTIN, THE GOVERNOR'S AGENT, TO THE RANI OF BOBBILI.

" MADAM,

Mr. Fraser, the Assistant Agent, has communicated to me that, in immediate response to his request, you despatched to Pachipenta fifty of your sepoys at a time when the Police were absent from that station. I am much obliged to you for your timely help.

* * * * *

(Signed) J. H. GARSTIN,
Agent to the Governor."

The Honourable the Maharajah Sir Venkata Sweta Chalapati Ranga Row Bahadur, K. C. I. E., who succeeded the Rani, was born on the 8th September 1862, at Venkatagiri, being the third son of no less a personage than H. H. the late Rajah Sarvagnya Kumarayachandra Bahadur Garu, C. S. I., the 27th in descent of the distinguished and well-known house of Venkatagiri.

When the Prince was nine years old, the House of Bobbili had no heir, but was under the guidance of Rani Lakshmi Chellayamma Bahadur Garu, who adopted him in 1872 as her heir and successor after the formal performance of the ceremonial rites observed in Hindu adoption. Arrangements befitting the position of the Rani were made for the education of the Prince, who, in spite of the most exalted position to which he had been raised, worked assiduously to acquire knowledge. He was first placed under the tuition of two competent native gentlemen, and when it was found that a European of good qualifications should be appointed tutor, the services of Mr. J. Marsh were secured, under whose guidance the Prince continued to be for nearly three years. During this period he received instruction not only in history, political economy and other subjects, but also in athletic exercises, in order to make him a man of good physique as well as a highly cultured ruler. The study of Sanskrit which contains the ethical code of the Hindus was not neglected, and a Pundit of rare attainments was employed to instil into the mind of the Prince the sacred principles of Hinduism. When he was fifteen years old, the title of "Empress" was conferred upon Her Majesty the late Queen Victoria. On that day, meetings, in commemoration of the unique event, were held at all the principalities in India. At the meeting that came off at Vizagapatam, the Prince took a conspicuous part and was given a seat on the *dais* with the late Maharajah of Vizianagram. One thing very remarkable connected with this noteworthy event was that the Princes of the two renowned houses which had been on hostile terms for years past met each other on the most friendly terms possible. It was on this most auspicious occasion that that seed of friendship was sown between the heads of the two distinguished families which, in process of time, grew into such a mighty fruit-bearing tree. The following year the installation of the Rajah of Venkatagiri, the Prince's eldest brother, took place, and at that ceremony was present the future ruler of Bobbili. It was on that auspicious occasion that the three sons of the Rajah of Venkatagiri who had been adopted to the three distinguished houses of Bobbili, Pittapur and Jetprole respectively, met one another, after having been separated for a long time. The same year the wedding of the Prince was celebrated at Bobbili on a grand scale, but the happy pair were destined to live in peace and harmony only for two years, as the Rani sank into an untimely grave in 1880, after giving birth to a son, Rajah Venkata Kumara Krishna Ranga Row Bahadur, the senior Kumararajah of Bobbili, the only fruit of their union. There is no rose but has its thorns and it was not, therefore, strange that some ill-feeling arose between the Prince and his adoptive mother, the Rani, but it did not exist long. At the intervention of Mr. Garstin, the then Collector of the Vizagapatam District, the way for reconciliation was paved, but he was suddenly transferred to another appointment, and the amicable settlement was brought about by the Honourable Mr. Carmichael, who was sent to Vizagapatam as a Special Commissioner in connection with the Rumpa Rebellion.

Before the Rajah was raised to the *gaddi*, he married his deceased wife's sister, as it was considered inauspicious for a widower to perform the ceremonial rites attendant on such occasions. The installation ceremony was performed on a magnificent scale on the 30th November 1881. He was very grateful to his adoptive mother, and it was his intention that the Rani should live without the least uneasiness in her mind, and he therefore set apart the revenue derived from the estate of Karakavalsa and some other villages, which amounted to Rs. 60,000, for the sole expenditure of the Rani.

The first and foremost reform which the Rajah set his hands to, was the raising of the Middle School of Bobbili to a High School on a constitutional basis, asking the Government of Madras to withdraw their grant. This reform, tending towards education, which was the first of a series of reforms introduced later on, speaks volumes in favor of the Rajah, whose educational attainments and liberal ideas imbibed under the fostering care of Mr. Marsh, have not been in vain, but have borne good fruit. The Rajah, not unmindful of the difficulties which the lame, the blind, and the decrepit are subject to, came forward to deserve a share of their gratitude by establishing a poor house. The moral and religious training he received while young, had made a deep impression upon his mind, and it was therefore his earnest desire that his subjects should also have the benefit of free exchange of thought; and with this object in view, he started an association for the discussion of religious, moral and scientific subjects.

Two years after the Rajah ascended the *guddi*, H. E. Sir M. E. Grant-Duff, the then Governor of Madras, visited Bobbili, and was the guest at the palace. Having entertained a very high opinion of the Rajah, His Excellency made the following remarks in the course of his reply to an address presented by the inhabitants of Bezwada :—

" We have in these North-eastern Districts men who, like the Maharajah of Vizianagram, the Zemindars of Mandasa, and of Bobbili, and the Rajah of Pittapur, are doing much in various ways for the enlightenment of those around them."

In 1883 the Rajah went on a pilgrimage to Benares, Gaya and other important places in Northern India, and after spending a few months in travel returned to his place. A sudden calamity that happened to him was the death of his second wife at child birth. This very nearly broke the heart of the Rajah, but he soon rallied, and resigned himself to the decrees of God. The following year he travelled to the chief towns of pilgrimage in Southern India, and before returning to Bobbili proceeded to Venkatagiri to witness the marriage festivities of his brother, the Rajah of Jetprole.

The death of the Rajah's adoptive mother, which melancholy event took place in 1887, was a heavy shock to him, and this was followed by the death of his younger son. The Rajah bore the losses with calm resignation.

The year 1887 has left a memorable page in the annals of the British Empire; the most noteworthy event of that year in which everybody, from prince to peasant, took part, was the Jubilee of Her Majesty, the late Empress of India. The Rajah, whose gratitude is as great as his loyalty to the British administration is beyond all doubt, in commemoration of the unique and auspicious event, erected a market at Bobbili, which was a desideratum for a long time, and designated it "The Victoria Market." In connection with this event the Rajah sent an address to the late august sovereign enclosing it in a silver casket.

In 1888 when the Rajah paid a visit to Madras he was rceived by Lord Marsham, an aid-de-camp to the Governor of Madras, with the usual respect to which a Rajah is entitled. There were visits to, and return visits from, the Governor. A few months afterwards the Rajah travelled to some of the important places in India, where he had the honor of interviews with H. R. H. the Duke of Connaught, H. E. Lord Dufferin, the then Viceroy, and H. E. Lord Reay, the then Governor of Bombay. This year a Question was raised as regards the hereditary titles to which the Rajah was entitled, and after a lenghly correspondence the title of "Rajah" which was held by his ancestors was recognised.

Among several other things, the *Madras Mail*, in commenting on the Birthday Honors, made the following remarks about the Rajah of Bobbili:—

"The Rajah is a young man of about 28, is a good horseman, and fond of sports and outdoor games. He is very popular with his ryots, and his careful administration of the affairs of the Zemindari has tended greatly to increase his revenue. He speaks and writes English with considerable ease. He is an enlightened and courteous nobleman who has travelled often and far, and made many friends in the three Presidencies."

The same year the Rajah married for the third time the present Maharani. He built a palace and styled it, "The Raj Mahal." The inside of the mansion is as varied and diversified in its arrangements as the exterior. The apartments are furnished in the most exquisite style. The gardens and adjacent grounds are laid out and arranged in the most tasteful and at the same time pleasant manner.

For more than three years there existed a dispute as regards the family property among the sons of the Rajah of Venkatagiri, the brothers of the Rajah of Bobbili. As the father and the brothers were alive to the fact that the Rajah was circumspect, able, and just, possessing the rare talent of conciliating the minds of men and of infusing a spirit of unanimity into a great number of discordant parties, they expressed their desire that he should be their arbitrator. The Rajah with his usual promptitude and willingness spared neither time nor pains in bringing about a reconciliation. In connection with this matter the following letter addressed by Lord Connemara under date 19th

August 1892, 106, Mount Street, Grosvenor Square, to the Rajah of Venkatagiri, proves the high opinion entertained of the Rajah of Bobbili by the noble lord :—

"MY DEAR RAJAH,

"I thank you for your letter of the 6th May, and I am very glad indeed to hear that the suit for a partition of your estate instituted by your father has been withdrawn. Family disputes are always especially disagreeable. Your brother, the Rajah of Bobbili, is a very sensible man, for whom I have a great regard, and has done well to interfere in this matter.

"With best good wishes for the welfare of all your family,

I remain,

Very sincerely yours,

(Signed) CONNEMARA."

On the 29th August of the same year the Rajah was blessed with a son, Sree Rajah Rama Krishna Ranga Row Bahadur, by his 3rd and present wife.

The Rajah attended the receptions at Madras, given to H. R. H. the late lamented Prince Albert Victor in 1889, and to His Imperial Highness the Czarewitch in 1891.

The year 1893 marks the most gratifying epoch in the reign of the Rajah, for it was in that year that he left on a voyage for Europe, accompanied by his youngest brother, Rajah Venugopaul Bahadur. On the 14th April, he left Bobbili, took steamer at Bombay and landed at Marseilles.

He visited Paris, and thence proceeded to London on the 19th May.

His Excellency the Governor, Lord Wenlock was kind enough to furnish him with letters of introduction to the Secretary of State for India and others. On the 29th of that month they attended the Levée at St. James' Palace held by His Royal Highness the Prince of Wales on Her Majesty's behalf. They were allowed the privilege of going to the Levée by the Ambassador's gate and were introduced by the Secretary of State for India. They also went to the customary Reception at the Foreign Office in honour of Her Majesty's Birth-Day on the 3rd June. They went by the Pimlico Entrance to the two State Balls and one State Concert given in Buckingham Palace. Having been invited by the Duke of Cambridge, they were present at the ceremony of laying the foundation-stone of the New Wing to the Royal United Service Institute, by H. R. H. the Prince of Wales. They paid their respects to H. R. H. the Duke of Connaught on the 19th July, when the Duke said he remembered seeing the Rajah at Poona. They also went to the Garden Party at Marlborough House, given on the 5th July by H. R. H. the Prince of Wales, to have the honour of meeting H. M. the Queen. Lord Kimberley, the Secretary of State for India, kindly introduced the Rajah and his brother to H. R. H. the Duke of York at the Garden Party given by Mr. and Lady Constance Shaw Lefevre to meet the Duke and Princess Victoria May before they were married. H. R. H. the Prince of Wales, at the interview given on the 10th July to the Rajah and his brother, was pleased to say that he was glad to make their acquaintance, to which the Rajah replied that it was a great honour to them to be graciously allowed to pay him their loyal respects. The Rajah paid his most humble and loyal respects to H. M. the Queen-Empress on the 17th July at Windsor Castle.

We deem it a great privilege to quote the following interesting account from the Rajah's diary:—

17TH "THE GREATEST DAY OF THE TOUR."

"I left my place at 20 minutes to 12 o'clock and drove to Paddington Station for Windsor Castle; thence I went in the Special train at 1-10 P.M., in which Lord Kimberley, Lord Ripon, and some other Privy Councillors were going to attend H. M.'s Council. Sir Gerald Fitzgerald met me at the station and accompanied me to the Castle. The Special train arrived at Windsor at 1-40 P.M. There were some carriages from the Castle awaiting to convey us there. Sir Fitzgerald and myself drove in a Landau drawn by a pair of horses which were driven by a postillion.

"In the Castle I was conducted to a room to wait there till called for. There I had some fruit and lemonade for my lunch. A little after 3 o'clock I was called for and was conducted by Sir Fitzgerald near to the Queen's Chamber. Then the Lord-in-waiting received me, conducted me to the Queen's Chamber, and presented me to Her Majesty. H. M. was standing, and shook hands with me in a very pleasing manner.

"Her Majesty's conversation, though short, was very kind and pleasing. Her Majesty was pleased to introduce me to H. M.'s daughter, Princess Beatrice of Battenberg, who was with Her Majesty.

"Through Her Majesty is 74 years of age, she noticed carefully my oriental costume. Her Majesty was very kind and pleasing in her expressions. I was very much pleased, and felt more honoured in being allowed thus to pay my most humble and loyal respects to our Sovereign who has already ruled 56 years. Since my boyhood I have had an intention to go to England to pay my loyal respects to Her Majesty. Now my wishes are realized.

"A few minutes after, the Privy Councillors and myself left the Castle, drove to the station, and returned to the Paddington station by the special train. Now I can say I am fully satisfied with my visit to this distant country. I may also mention here in this connection that I am the first Rajah that has ever come from the Madras Presidency.

"Thank God ! this is the most happy day of my life."

Shortly afterwards the Rajah was presented with a photo bearing H. M.'s autograph signature, in acknowledging the receipt of which the Rajah wrote as follows :—

"I have no words to express my most humble and loyal thanks to Her Gracious Majesty, the Queen and Empress of India, for H. M.'s most kind favour in presenting me with Her Portrait. I esteem it a very great and special favour on the part of H. M. to my ancient family which had been ever loyal to the British Government and whose footsteps, it has been, and will ever be, my desire to follows :—

"I have erected a market at Bobbili, to commemorate H. M.'s Jubilee, and on my return to my country, I intend to build a Town Hall in memory of my loyal visit to H. M., which, with H. M.'s permission, I would name the 'Victoria Town Hall.'

"I would beg you, Sir, to convey to Her Gracious Majesty, with every expression of loyalty, and with my humble thanks, my gratitude for, and appreciation of, H. M.'s Gracious Gift.

I have the honour to remain,

Sir,

Your most obedient and humble servant,

(Signed) V. S. RANGA ROW,

Rajah of Bobbili."

In reply to this the Right Hon'ble H. F. Ponsonby wrote:—

"OSBORNE, ISLE OF WIGHT

ENGLAND,

17*th August,* 1893.

"SIR,

"In reply to your letter, which I had much pleasure in submitting to the Queen, I am commanded by Her Majesty to assure you that she has learnt with much satisfaction your intention of building a Town Hall, in memory of your visit to the Queen, and that Her Majesty gladly grants permission for the building to be named the 'Victoria Town Hall.'

I have the honour to be,

Sir,

Your faithful servant,

(Signed) HENRY F. PONSONBY."

The Rajah presented an ivory casket to H. R. H. the Princess May of Teck, as a wedding present, which was acknowledged in the following words:—

WHITE LODGE,
RICHMOND PARK,
SURREY.

"Her Serene Highness the Princes Victoria May of Teck, desires the Comptroller to convey her greatful thanks to H. H. the Rajah of Bobbili for the beautiful gift he has kindly sent to her which the Princess has pleasure in accepting."

4th July, 1893.

The Rajah subscribed 100 guineas to St. Mary's Hospital Fund, and presented an ivory casket to the Queen-Empress. He and his brother attended the "At Homes" of the Duke of Westminster, the Marchioness of Salisbury, Lady Battersea, Lady Henry Lennox, and the Marchioness of Ripon, the Countess of Jersey, and also Lady Temple's Garden Party and the Anniversary Fête at the Crystal Palace.

He visited Lord Kimberley, Secretary of State for India, Lord Connemara, Sir Mountstuart Grant-Duff, Lord Herschell, Lord Northbrook, Lord Reay, and some others.

At the public functions he was also introduced to H. R. H. Princess Christian, H. R. H. the Duke of Cambridge, the Duke of Teck, Lord Dufferin, Lord Roberts, and many others.

During his sojourn in England, the Rajah visited Brighton, Oxford, Liverpool, Edinburgh, and Bedford.

On the 22nd August he set sail from England and visited Paris, Lucerne, Venice, Florence, and Rome, embarked on the S.S. *Shannon* at Brindisi for India on the 19th, and reached Bombay on the 2nd September, following:—

He received addresses of welcome from the people of Venkatagiri, and of Bobbili where he safely returned on the 13th September 1893.

The impression made upon the English public by the Rajah was deep and is sure to be lasting. He attracted universal regard by his personal qualities as well as by his exalted rank. The respect he received in England was directed as much to the man as to the prince and his discriminating mind felt the tribute, while his heart perhaps acknowledged it as the most grateful regard to which his services for his subjects were entitled.

In 1894, in commemoration of his recent visit to England, the Rajah built a hall, called the "Victoria Town Hall," the foundation stone of which was laid by H. E. Lord Wenlock, the then Governor of Madras, who, after performing the ceremony, addressed those present as follows:—

"I feel great pleasure in acceding to the request made by you to lay the foundation-stone here in commemoration of the visit which you paid to Her Majesty the Queen-Empress when you visited England last year. I do not think that you could possibly commemorate this visit in a more suitable and proper manner than that in which you propose to do. It is therefore a matter of extreme pleasure and satisfaction to myself that I have been able to come here on this occasion, and perform the ceremony of laying the foundation-stone of what, I trust, will be the lasting record of loyalty to Her Most Gracious Majesty the Queen-Empress, and of your devotion to her, and the loyal principles with which you and your family have always been associated. I believe this particular form which you have chosen is one most suitable to the people of this country. They will find in this building, which you are about to erect, opportunities of meeting on occasions when their deliberations can be properly accompanied by suitable surroundings, such as are going to be placed at their disposal as a record of not only your own loyalty, but of the generosity and interest which you feel towards ameliorating the condition of your own people. It is for these and other reasons that I am pleased to be here this afternoon and I shall be glad to send home an account of my visit here, and to assure all those at home who have, as I have, a lively interest in all matters connected with this country, that they will find, here in Bobbili, a nobleman who is anxious to do his duty to all by whom he is surrounded and who is anxious to prove on all occasions his loyalty and affection to Her Majesty the Queen-Empress. With these words I can do no more than congratulate you on this auspicious occasion, and I trust it will not be long before the building is erected which will be a lasting record of events, which have been of such satisfaction and gratification to yourself, and to those who are, as I am, interested in the welfare and well-being of the people of this country."

At the entertainment given at the Raj Mahal, His Excellency the Governor proposed the Rajah's health thus:—

"Rajah, Ladies, and Gentlemen,—I have to thank you, Sir, very much indeed for the kind manner in which you have proposed my health, and those who have also received what you have proposed just now in an extremely touching manner. I can only say for myself that it is a matter of extreme pleasure to me that I have been able to respond to the invitation that you were kind enough to extend to me some time ago, *viz.*, that I should come to Bobbili towards the end of this year to lay the stone which I had the honour of doing this afternoon. * *

" * * * Here is a town and an estate administered in the most excellent and most practical manner. I gather, from every source which is open to me to obtain information from, that the people of this country are happy and enjoying themselves in quiet and prosperity, and that you keep a special watch and special guard over their interests in a most special manner. On behalf of Government I can only express my sincere thanks for the manner in which you look after all those in whom you are interested, and amongst whom your work is cast. The ceremony that I had the honour of being present at this afternoon was a specially interesting one, as it was one commemorating the visit which you yourself paid to Her Majesty the Queen-Empress, when you were in England; it is one which will hand down to posterity a record of that visit, and specially of the loyal spirit which was predominating in your own mind at the time when you paid your visit to that country. I think I may safely say that, in the Northern Circars, Landlords and Zemindars of this country are animated by the same spirit which animated you, and if, at any time, their fortune should be so great that they should be able to pay their respects, in the same manner as you did, to Her Majesty the Queen-Empress, they will be actuated by the same feelings of loyalty and devotion to the British Crown as you yourself, Sir, possess. I do not know if it is necessary for me to say anything more than, on behalf of Government, to thank you for the extremely kind hospitality which you have extended to us, and which has made our visit so very comfortable and so very enjoyable."

* * * * *

The following day, His Excellency, on behalf of Lady Wenlock, laid the foundation stone of the Samasthanam Gosha Hospital, and spoke thus:—

"RAJAH,—I can only express to you my great pleasure in acceding to the request which you have made that I should attend the ceremony of laying the foundation-stone of this hospital, and at the same time of assuring you of the great regret which Lady Wenlock feels at not being able to be present here and perform the ceremony which I have just undertaken. * * *

* * * * *

"Your own family has contributed largely in this particular direction. The Gosha Hospital at Madras, the gift, almost the entire gift of the Rajah of Venkatagiri, shows very well how keenly the members of your family take interest in this particular matter. The foundation of this institution here shows that you yourself are as keenly alive to the interests of those unfortunate women of this country, who, up till now, have received so little support. I hope this institution, when it is once started, will be the means of affording relief and comfort to a very large number of women of this country and this town;

and that other bodies and private individuals, who come to see the good work here done, will not hesitate to follow your excellent example.

* * * * *

"I have only to express the pleasure I have had in being here, and to congratulate you on the extremely good example you have set to others, who, like yourself, are responsible for the well-being of such a large number of persons."

The Rajah built the Gosha Hospital and the Lady Apothecary's quarters at Bobbili at his own cost, and handed them over to the District Board with a magnificent donation of Rs. 20,000 for the management and up-keep of the institution.

The Rajah was very much indebted to Mr. Turner, a former Collector of the Vizagapatam District for the friendly advice he always gave him, and it was therefore his intention to pay some tribute to his memory in a substantial manner, and when the Rajah threw out his suggestion to build a choultry, it took a definite shape, and contributions came from the people of the District, the list being headed by the Rajah with Rs. 6,000.

The Rajah was kinghted in 1895, when the following observations ware made by the *Madras Mail* :—

"Among the recipients of higher honours the only Madras name that appears is that of the Rajah of Bobbili. This nobleman has exhibited progressive tendencies of a marked kind. He has, like several of his *confreres* in other parts of India, overcome the aversion to undertaking a voyage to England. Since his return, he has been endeavouring to show that the experience gained has had the effect of enlarging his mind. Lord Wenlock, during his recent tour in the Northern Circars, laid the foundation-stones of two important and much-needed institutions which the Rajah himself admitted were in commemoration of his visit."

The ceremony of investiture took place at Ootacamund. H. E. Lord Wenlock, the then Governor of Madras, invested the Rajah with the insignia of the Most Exalted Order of the Indian Empire. In addition to the honor conferred upon the Rajah by the British Government and the kind words said of him by the Governor, all his subjects without one dissentient voice resolved to offer to their beloved Rajah the highest tribute of respect and praise that could be bestowed upon a Prince. The Rajah, on returning to Bobbili, was the recipient of a spontaneous address from all classes of his subjects. While thanking them for their kindness, he said that he could not carry out all their requests at once but promised to fulfil many of them in due course. On this occasion he showed his generosity by remitting to his subjects, Rs. 30,000, arrears of revenue.

The Rajah paid his respects to H. E. Lord Elgin, the then Viceroy, when His Excellency visited Madras, and he then endowed a bed to be called, "Lady Elgin's bed" in the Victoria Caste Gosha Hospital in Madras. In 1896 the Rajah endowed another bed to be called "Lady Wenlock's bed."

When the seat in the Governor's Council occupied by the late Maharajah of Vizianagram fell vacant on the expiry of his term, the then Governor of Madras nominated the Rajah to it.

In the famine of 1896-97 the Rajah subscribed Rupees 10,000, to the Indian Famine Relief Charitable Fund, fed a vast multitude of poor people in the Samasthanam Poor House, spent about Rs. 25,000 on irrigation works, and sold grain at a very low rate to the Samasthanam servants and to the poor of all classes.

In 1897 the Diamond Jubilee of Her Majesty the late Queen Empress was celebrated with great *eclat* at Bobbili. A durbar was held, a large concourse of people being present at it. The Rajah evinced his loyalty and attachment to the British power by sending an address to Her Majesty enclosing it in a suitable casket.

On the 21st February 1898 the "Victoria Town Hall" was opened by H. E. Lord Havelock. The following felicitous speech was made on the occasion by the Governor:—

"The Rajah has so fully and clearly explained the history and objects of this Town Hall that there remains little for me to say except that I feel it a pleasure and honour to be asked to consummate the work which was begun by my distinguished predecessor. I appreciate very heartily and deeply the sentiments which have moved the Rajah to carry out this work, and I trust that the usefulness of the building with which he has endowed the Town of Bobbili will be extensive and long-lasting. With these words I now declare the Victoria Town Hall to be duly opened."

The people of the Town and the Zemindari presented an address to His Excellency, and received a reply from him at the Town Hall. In his reply he said :—

"**Representatives of people of the Town of Bobbili.**—I thank you for your kind address of welcome.

It is with the greatest satisfaction I have heard the tribute of praise which you have bestowed upon the Rajah of Bobbili who, as you say, has endowed you with many useful public institutions, and they are valuable works to that extent. You admit that you are supplied with schools, hospitals, and other charitable institutions, and that water-supply has been amply provided for. This is a very high tribute of gratitude and praise to your enlightened Rajah. In consequence of his munificence towards you, you say that there is very little left for you to ask at my hands. * * * * *

I am glad to be able to join with you in congratulating ourselves on the success of the efforts of the Government to withstand the horrors of famine and distress during last year. I take this opportunity of expressing the gratitude of the Government for the efforts that were made by the Rajah himself to assist the people in his own immediate neighbourhood, and I wish also not to lose this opportunity of expressing the high appreciation of my Government of the skill, zeal and devotion of the District Officers under extremely difficult and trying circumstances. I thank you once more for the welcome you have accorded to me here."

In proposing the health of the Rajah at the entertainment given to His Excellency in the evening of the same day, the latter spoke thus :—

"I thank you, Rajah, for the kind and too flattering terms in which you have proposed the toast of my health. I thank you, gentlemen, also for having so cordially responding to it. It is true, as the Rajah remarked, that the determining cause of my visit to the Circars was his invitation to take part in the ceremony of opening the Hall, the ceremony which I look forward to performing to-morrow. I had the intention of coming to this part of the country during this season if it had been possible. But for my promise to take part in this ceremony, I think, I should have been compelled to postpone it to a future occasion. However, I have managed to find sufficient time to carry out the projected visit to this part of the country, and I am very glad to find myself to-night as the guest of the Rajah. I am certain that Lady Havelock would have been pleased, if she could, with her presence on the present occasion, have given an additional satisfaction to the Rajah. But the Rajah has rightly said that the long journey from Madras, performed in the hurried way that my journey on the present occasion was arranged to be performed, prevented her from coming. She could not possibly have undergone the fatigues of this long and hasty journey. Before I sit down, I must ask you to join with me in drinking a toast which probably needs little or no commendation, that is, the toast of the health of the Rajah of Bobbili. The Rajah of Bobbili is, as we all know, a descendant and a representative of the race which has distinguished itself in the wars in this part of the country, and has left its mark on the history of the Circars. The Rajah himself is a man of literary ability; he has also been an observant traveller; he is a large landowner who knows how to work his property to the best possible advantage, and he is, I can testify, a most valuable member of my Legisative Council, representing there the interests of the large landed proprietary of the Madras Presidency. I can only say that I wish that we had many more men in the Madras Presidency and in India like the Rajah of Bobbili."

The *Madras Mail* remarked thus on the speeches made by H. E. the Governor and the Rajah Bahadur :—

" It will be seen from the reports we publish to-day that the Governor's visit to Bobbili was marked by some very cordial speech-making. Referring to His Excellency the Rajah remarked :—

" It is a rare fortune for a Province to be presided over by such a statesman, a statesman who, by a life which has been devoted to his country's service, has added to the high gifts of nature, a vast store of practical knowledge and experience, and who, while he is ready to listen to the popular voice and official advice, is at the same time capable of maintaining his own independence of judgment."

In the middle of April the wedding of the Kumara Rajah of Bobbili was celebrated with much rejoicing. The Rajah's mother, the Rajah of Venkatagiri, K. C. I. E., Rajah Muddu Kristna with his wife, and Rajah Venkata Krishna came from Venkatagiri. Rajah Venugopala Krishna and the second son of the Kumara Rajah of Pittapur also arrived from Madras. The Zemindar of Sangamvalsa was also present at the wedding.

The Rajah was renominated to the Legislative Council in 1898, and he has since then been a member of that august assembly. No objection was raised to his election, which was felt to be well deserved, whilst there seemed to be every probability that his habits of business would be advantageously brought into play. He expressed his views more freely than ever against the Tenancy Bill, and thus fully realized the confidence reposed in him by his constituents.

There was a sudden bereavement in the noble family of Bobbili in May 1899, caused by the death of the great-grand mother of the Rajah at the ripe old age of 90 years. The venerable lady was very fortunate, indeed, as she lived to see her grandson's grandson. The Rajah endowed a third bed in the Victoria Caste and Gosha Hospital in the name of the deceased grand old lady.

On the 22nd of October 1899 the Kumara Rajah was blessed with a daughter; she is the first grandchild of the Rajah. She was named in November, "Sree Victoria Vencata Ramanamma." The name of Victoria was selected by the Rajah to show his admiration, love, and respect for Her Majesty the late Queen-Empress.

In 1899 the personal distinction of "Maharajah" was conferred by the Government of India on the Rajah of Bobbili.

The Maharajah was selected by the Government of Madras to represent the aristocracy of Southern India on the occasion of the Coronation of His Majesty King Edward VII. The Maharajah went to England, was present at the ceremony, paid his respects to His Majesty, and returned some months ago after visiting many places of importance in Europe. There was a grand send off and great ovation when he left Bobbili for England, and on returning safe, there was a warm reception and kind welcome by his ryots. There was the usual presentation of addresses to the Maharajah.

It is an admitted fact that the Maharajah of Bobbili has won the confidence and esteem of the Government of Madras by the successful manner in which he has been managing the estate. His warm heart, his open hand, his free and cordial manner, have won the love of his ryots. His courteousness and affability have secured him many noble friends both among Europeans and natives.

H. H. The Maharaja of Jeypore.

Kallikote Estate Press, Rambha.

H. H. THE MAHARAJAH OF JEYPORE

(*VIZAGAPATAM DISTRICT*).

His Highness the Maharajah, Sri Sri Sri Vikrama Deo, Azem, Maharajah, Yujadud Dowla, Mahabat Assar, Yedal Yemeenay, Salatnut, Samsamay, Killapathay, Islam Sri Jhadkhand Badusha, Maharajah of Jeypore, of the Solar Race, the possessor of a hilly tract, in the Vizagapatam District, naturally mild and pacific like his father, possesses a quick apprehension and extensive capacity, evinces talents for business, and is no less distinguished for sobriety and decorum of deportment than for literary acquirements. He ascended the *guddi* at a time when all animosities had begun to subside and tranquility reigned supreme throughout the Samastanam. The prudent conduct of his father had removed the principal obstacle which had embarrassed his predecessors; and to maintain the tranquility so happily established required no arduous exertions of body or of mind, no daring enterprise or complicated scheme of policy, but the same mixture of prudence, moderation and firmness as characterised his father's administration.

Jeypore Samastanam is in the Vizagapatam District, Madras Presidency, lying between 17 30' and 20° N. Lat. and 81° 20' and 84° 4 Long. It is bounded on the north by Kalahundi in the Central Provinces; on the east by the plain of Vizagapatam; on the south by Rekapally and Golconda; on the west by Bastar. The area of the Samastanam is 11,526 square miles and population, 4,42,454.

The Jeypore Samastanam is divided into two parts, Upper and Lower, which are within the jurisdictions of the Special and Senior Assistant Agents, whose Head-Quarters are at Koraput and Parvatipur respectively.

To the east and north-east of Gunupur lies the Savra Hill Country, consisting of two table-lands about 200 square miles in extent. North of Gunupur the Samastanam runs up in a wedge-like form to a distance of 70 miles between Kalahundi of the Central Provinces on the west, and Parlakimidy on the east reaching very nearly 20° N. Lat. In the centre of this district stands out the remarkable group of hills named Nimghiris which rise to a height of 5000 feet separated by the valley of not more than 1200 feet from the ranges on either hand. The drainage from Nimghiries and the neighbouring countries flows directly south-east to the sea, forming at Kalingapatam, the river Vamsadhara, so called from the bamboos, (vamsa) growing on its banks and the Nagavali at Chicacole. The population chiefly Khonds and Sawras number 1,37,966, the largest towns being Jeypore, Kotpad, Nowrangpur, Nandapur, Gudari, Gunupur, Rayaghada, Singapur and Bissamkatak. The western portion of the country consists of the taluks of Jeypore, Nowrangapur, and Malkanagiri, while the taluk of Koraput lies in the east. The principal towns are Jeypore, Kotpad and Nowrangapur.

The religion of the country is mainly Hinduism. Ethnologically the inhabitants include Aryans, Colarians, and Dravidians. The Aryans are comparatively recent colonists and comprise the ruling and fighting men and the priests. The cultivators called Purajas (literally subjects) number about more than two-thirds of the entire population, Aryans represent one-seventeenth, Parjas one-sixth. The mountaineers retain far greater independence than the ryots of the Jeypore and the Malakanagiri plateaus. In the uplands patriarchal authority is still unassailable; in the low-lying lands it is only preserved in parts where jungle tracts abound which are being slowly brought under cultivation.

The Maharajah is the rightful owner of the land. Every variety of land tenure is found throughout Jeypore. The tenants have no occupancy right. When the Maharajah is satisfied as to the advisability of leasing out the land to a stranger, he has a legal right to do so. The pattas and muchalkas exchanged between the Maharajah and his tenants are yearly documents and they contain express stipulations binding the tenants to relinquish their right to the lands at the end of the Fasli.

The religious ceremonies and social customs of the various tribes differ but little from one another. The process of fusion of the habits of the later immigrants with aboriginal customs is, however, very apparent. In those parts of the country which are in a prosperous condition ideas and manners imported from the coast districts are gradually overcoming and absorbing all aboriginal conceptions, but on the other hand, in jungle-covered and backward lands the colonists are always corrupted by the superstitions of the indigenous races. The following is Mr. Carmichael's account of the Zemindary tenure :—

"At the period of the cession of the Northern Circars we found the country divided into Navili and Zemindari. The Navili lands consisted of the old domestic or household lands of the sovereign and tracts near to towns resumed by the Muhammadans and appropriated for the support of their numerous garrisons and establishments. These lands the local Foujdars and Nawabs always retain under their immediate management parcelling out the rest of the country into Zemindaries. But the Muhammadan rulers were impatient of details and a mode was invented of transacting the business of revenue more in the gross. Their revenue agents were rendered stationary in the districts where they collected and became responsible to Government for revenue, receiving payment by a percentage or share of what they collected. Under native governments every thing which was enjoyed, whether office or possession, had a tendency to become hereditary. There was a convenience in preserving in each district the same agent of revenue, and after him, his son or successor, because each was better acquainted with the people and the resources of the district than, generally speaking, any other man could be. In this manner the situation of these agents became in fact hereditary, and before the period of the English acquisitions, the Persian appellation of Zemindar had been generally appropriated by them. The Jeypore Zemindari and the family of its Rajah are of old standing, and the origin of both is involved in a mist of tradition.

"Previous to the acquisition of the Northern Circars by the East India Company, Jeypore was paying tribute to Hyderabad.

"In 1848, the affairs of the Samastanam fell into a great confusion owing to the insubordination of some members of the Maharajah's family. The disturbance went so far that Lower taluks were attached by the Government. The troubles lasted two years and broke out again in

1385. In 1860, for the 1st time, the British interefered in the administration."

Jeypore (Jeypuram, "the city of victory"), town in the Jeypore Samastanam, Vizagapatam District, Madras Presidency, Lat 88° 55' N, and Long. 82° 83' is situated at an elevation of about 2,000 feet above the sea 7 miles to the north of the northern wall of the plateau of the Vizagapatam hills.

The Royal family of Jeypore traces its origin to Jammu (Cashmere) and to a date many centuries ago. Kumbhirajah Deo a descendant of Kanakasena of the solar race was once the King of Jammu. He had three sons and the second of them, Vinaik Deo, who could not succeed his father, while the eldest son was alive, repaired to Benares on a pilgrimage, where it is traditionally believed he made a penance and after twenty, one days of hard and rigid penance the god, Kasi Wisweswar, appeared in his dream, and bade him go to Nandapur, telling him at the same time that he would obtain the throne of that kingdom. In obedience to the mandate of Kasi Wisweswar, Vinaik Deo left at once for Nandapur. The journey to that place was not easy then, for there were not so many facilities for travel as there are now; nevertheless, he did not feel the wearines of travel, as the enterprise he had embarked on was such that if he should achieve his object he would be raised to a high position. He would be an independent king ruling over a large state with a number of feudal lords under his control. As the journey was anything but pleasant, he underwent many difficulties and privations, and ultimately reached the place whither he was enjoined to proceed without delay by god, Kasi Wisweswar. On reaching the place, he enterd the temple dedicated to Sarweswar; and in the course of his usual prayer, he mentioned the object of his visit to the place. The very night, the god, Sarweswar, appeared in a dream to the king of Nandapur, and said that an accomplished prince was present at the temple, and that he was by far the best qualified to receive the hand of his (King's) daughter. This was a surprise to the latter but as he had had no male issue he thought that he had better make the prince his son-in-law, should he be endowed with all the accomplishments as detailed by the god in the dream. With this resolve he went to the temple where, to his surprise and wonder, he beheld the prince dressed shabbily. The coarse garments were lost sight of in the contemplation of his fine form, his upright gait and the intellectual cast of his countenance. After mature deliberation, the King arrived at the conclusion that, as regards the new-comer the prince and his daughter the princess, should he resolve to unite their hands, there would be no circumstance to raise a suspicion of an inequality of social grades to present an insuperable barrier to their union. The prince related to the King the circumstances that took him to the place; thereupon the latter took the former to his house and made him his son-in-law, entrusting to him the management of the State. The new king, named Vinaik Singh Deo, governed the place by a strict adherence to the laws then in existence and by a mixture of moderation and firmness he succeeded in maintaining the peace. For some reason or other, the people of the place rose against him and as he was unable to subdue their turbulence, he had no other alternative than to attempt to find his way back to his native country. In his wanderings he came in contact with one Bonijaro (merchant) Naik, by name Lobinia, who helped the prince with an army consisting of cavalry, and infantry, and 10,000 cattle for transport. With this equipment, Vinaik King Deo proceeded again to Nandapur, quelled the rebellion and took possession of the kingdom. In token of gratitude to the merchant prince whose help was most opportune, Vinaik Singh Deo used in his signature *chatuni* (a rope used by the merchants for tying cattle). This mark has from that time forward been used by all the succeeding kings. Vianik Sing Deo went against many kingdoms and conquered them. The boundaries of the then Nandapur Samastanam were as follow :—

East.—Up to Chicacole.
South. ,, ,, Rayavaram in Sarvasiddi Taluq.
West. ,, ,, Bhaskali river and Bastar.
North. ,, ,, Budalingam beyond Kalahandi, and Pota-Chinchada near Boda Kimidi and Gummagodo near Parlakimidi.

Viñaik Singh Deo reigned for 33 years and died in the year 1476. He was succeeded by his son Sri Viziachandraksha Deo who reigned for 34 years and died in 1510. It was during his reign that the Goddess Sri Kanaka Durga and the God Sri Vallabhanarayanaswamy were brought from the Carnatic and established in the Nandapur town. The next in succession was Sri Bhariva Deo, who was born in 1486, and ascended the throne in 1510, in his 24th year. The large tank which goes by the name of Bhairava Sagar in Bobbili owes its existence to him.

Sri Viswanadha Deo who succeeded him reigned for a long period of 44 years but his rule was marked by no event of importance. His son, Sri Balarama Deo who held the reins of administration for over a quarter of a century followed in the wake of his father by introducing no changes in the administration and by adhering to the principles laid down by his ancestors. His son, Sri Yesovanta Deo became king at the comparatively young age of 16 and reigned for 40 years. The following rule was characterised by events of some importance. Sri Vikrama Deo, the king, transferred his capital from Nandapur to Jeypore where he erected a fort. The Nizam of Golconda (Hyderabad) presented the king with a sword, mohee-morath (nishanees) and an elephant with a yellow *howdha*, conferring on him the following titles :—

"Azem Maharajah, Yujadud-Dowla, Mahabat-Assar, Yedal-Yemeenay,Salatnut-Samasamay, Khillapathay,Islam Sree Jhadkhand Badusha Jeypore Circar."

The Sunnad conferring the said titles, and the presents referred to above are still preserved in the Jeypore fort as relics.

Sri Vikrama Deo had two wives. It was at the time of the marriage of the king with the junior Rani that the country lying between Gummagodo and Kiny villages was alienated to the Parlakimidy family. Sri Krishna Deo, the son by the senior Maharani came to the throne in 1669. He reigned for a short time, and it was during this period that Poosapati Seetaramarazu, who came from Bezwada was given Kumili and Gandredu, and the following Zemindaries were created :—Bobbili, Devupalli, Rekapalli, Narava Mutha, Kottakki and Salur.

The next in right of succession was Sri Viswambhara Deo Maharajah who reigned only for four years from 1672 to 1676. It was during this Maharajah's time that the following Zemindaries were formed :—Pedapadam,

Ramabhadrapuram, Makkuva, Sividi, Kurapam, Merangi, Palem Mutha, Palakonda, Birikotu, Pachipenta, Poram, Rangavalasa, Andra, Koduru, Sambam, Bondapilly, Kalahundi, Bindra Novogodo, and Khariar; and officers were appointed for the administration of these Zemindaries.

There was now a break in the line of succession as the last mentioned Maharajah died issueless, while each of the former Maharajahs had a son to succeed him. However, Sri Viswambhara Deo Maharajah had a brother Sri Mallakimardhana Krishna Deo who came to the throne in 1676. He fought with the French and succeeded in capturing some of their guns at Nandapur. His brother Sri Hari Deo Maharajah reigned only for three years and found an untimely grave in 1684. Sri Balarama Deo, the brother of the former Maharajah who came to the throne in 1684, adopted Sri Raghunath Krishna Deo, the grand son of his uncle Sri Yesovanta Deo of Gunupur. Sri Raghunatha Deo Maharajah's reign extended over 20 years, and the only event of importanee was that Bissamkatak and Merangi were made tributaries. After the demise of the Maharajah, his son Sri Ramachandra Deo Maharajah was placed at the head of the administration. It was at his instance that the Sangamvalasa Zemindari was established. The last days of the Maharajah were any thing but pleasant to him as family dissensions and quarrels weighed heavy on his heart. He died childless, and his brother Sri Balarama Deo, who was the main cause of the family disputes became ruler in 1711. He was very unfortunate as he ruled the State only for a couple of years. Before he breathed his last, he had the pleasure to see the Zemindaries of Kalahundi and Khariar and Nuvagodo gaining independence under the auspices of the

Maharattas. He was succeeded by his brother Sri Viswambhara Deo Maharajah who ascended the throne in 1713. He was a typical orthodox Hindu. It was he that established the Ugratara Yentra and the Goddess China Kanaka Durga in Jeypore. The next in succession was Sri Lala Krishna Deo the step-brother of the former Maharajah, who ruled over the Samastanam for a period of six years, and finding every thing in chaos, betook himself to Kalayanasingapur. His brother Sri Vikrama Deo Maharajah came to the throne in 1758. He was assisted in the administration by the well-known Dewan Jagannadhapatro. It was during the rule of this Maharajah that fierce battles took place, one of them being against the French at Malkanagiri; they were driven away as far as Godavery. Another battle that followed was with the Maharattas at Ummerkota. The payment of Jamabandi which was hitherto made to the Nizam of Hyderabad was transferred to the British, and the Parganas of Kotpad were acquired from Bastar for the military assistance rendered to the Bastar king in 1777.

Sri Ramachandra Deo Maharajah ascended the throne in 1779. He reigned nearly for half a century; during which long period the Peish-cush payable to the paramount power was fixed at Rs. 16,000 and an elephant with four horses was presented to the Maharajah by the Nagpur Government. The living monuments of his long reign are the Jagannasagar tank in Jeypore, the Mekhamala and other gardens, the Jagannadhapur and Ganganapur Agraharams. The custom Sati being in existence then, the third wife of the Mahrajah ascended the funeral pile with her husband. The British Government issued to the Maharajah a *Sannad Milkiet Istimirar*.

Sri Vikrama Deo Maharajah, the son of Sri Ramachandra Deo Maharajah, came to the throne in 1825. His administrative capacity was so great that immediately after he assumed the reins of Government he instituted such wholesome measures that he found it a light task to change the chaos into order and to infuse a new spirit into the *personnel* of the State. Several futuridars whose heads turned and who always troubled the former Maharajahs were arrested and brought to book. He was very pious and orthodox. Up to this time the administration of Criminal and Civil justice was practically in the hands of the Maharajahs of this family.

Sri Ramachandra Deo Maharajah who was born in 1843 assumed the reins of administration in 1860. He rendered valuable aid to the British Government in quelling the Savra rising in the Gunupur taluq and the well-known Rampa rebellion in the Godavery District. The authorities, while placing on record their high appreciation of the attachment of the Maharajah, went to the extent of presenting him with a sword, a military uniform, a diamond ring, a rifle, a watch and a pearl necklace. When H. R. H. the Prince of Wales, now King Edward VII, visited Madras, the Maharajah was one of those that were introduced to his Royal Highness, who presented him with a medal. Several educated men, Brahmins and Muhammadans, who hailed from distant places, found in him a great patron. It would appear that in 1860 the Maharajah voluntarily resigned the administration of Civil and Criminal justice in favour of the British.

The present Maharajah, Sri Sri Sri Vikrama Deo, was born in 1875, and as he was a minor of 14 years at the time of his father's death, the management of the

Samastanam was taken over by Government. When the prince arrived at the years of discretion, his father made suitable arrangements for the education of the son and Dr. Marsh who was then appointed tutor remained as such till the expiration of the minority of the prince. Sri Vikrama Deo attained under his tuition a considerable degree of learning and a general knowledge of the arts and sciences. True to the principle that travelling is half education, the doctor took his pupil to almost all the places of importance in India. In the course of these tours, he interviewed Lord Elgin, the then Viceroy and Governor-General of India, and Lord Wenlock, the then Governor of Madras. Under the most favourable auspices, after the Maharajah had received a sound education and the Government of Madras had formed a high opinion of his character, Sri Sri Sri Vikrama Deo Maharajah ascended the *guddi* on the 27th November 1895. It was a day of very great rejoicing to the people of Jeypore to find the son of their deceased Maharajah, with all the accomplishments necessary for a ruler of a large Samastanam, placed at the head of the administration. The investiture ceremony took place at the instance of Mr. Willock, I.C.S., the then Agent to the Governor at Vizagapatam, when all the local European and Native Officials were present to witness the inauguration. In 1893 the Maharajah was married to a princess of the well-known Surgoja House in Udayapur (Chota Nagapur). The fruit of this union is Sri Sri Sri Ramachandra Deo born on the 17th December 1893. The Government of India in recognition of the merit and qualifications of the Prince conferred on him the personal distinction of *Maharajah* in 1896, which was originally owned by his ancestors both before and after the advent of the British. The Maharajah went to Madras in

The Kumara Rajah of Jeypore.

Kallikote Estate Press, Rambha.

1901 and visited His Excellency Lord Curzon, the Viceroy and Governor-General of India, and also Sir Arthur Havelock, the then Governor of Madras. He again visited Madras in January 1902 and had an interview with Lord Ampthill the present Governor. The construction of the new fort which was commenced during his minority was completed by him. After assuming the reins of the Samastanam, he made grand improvements to the old fort now in the occupation of the Royal Family. A temple was lately constructed by Her Highness Lakshmi Devi Rajeswari, the Dowager Maharani, at a cost of 70,000 Rupees and dedicated to the god Ramachandraswami.

Be it said to the credit of the Maharajah that he opens his purse liberally to any institution that is calculated to do good to the public at large. He is not conservative, but is very liberal although he may be said to be orthodox. We are glad to observe that he has offered Rs. 150,000 to the Government of Madras for the construction of the Collab and the Indravati bridges. To the Victoria Memorial Hall Fund at Calcutta, he lately gave Rs. 5,000, and a similar amount to the same fund at Madras. The Maharajah and the Maharani Circar have established four beds in Victoria Caste and Ghosha Hospital at a cost of Rs. 8,800. The Maharajah sometime ago subscribed and paid Rs. 4,000 to the Indian Famine Relief Fund and 1,050 Rupees to the Transvaal War Fund. Through Mr. H. A. Sim, the Maharajah paid Rs. 1,500 to the Royal Asiatic Society's Medal Fund in England, and to the Victoria Memorial Hall Redemption Fund in Madras, Rs. 1,500.

He pays the following annual contributions to the Government of Madras :—

			RS.
Agency Works	...	...	10,000
Vaccination	...	...	1,800
Medical ...	...	...	700
Sanitation ...	...	...	750
Education ...	...	...	1,200

The Maharajah is aided in the affairs of the Samastanam by M. R. Ry. P. Venkannah Pantulu Garu, who after having made a name as a revenue officer of extraordinary abilities in the British service, joined the staff of the Samastanam some years ago. It is gratifying to find that the Samastanam has an efficient establishment and the following are the Officers thereof :—

Durbar Sanskrit Pandits.

1. M.R.Ry. Vidyabhushana Kristna Nando Sastri Garu.
2. M.R.Ry. Krishna Dass Garu.

Family Purohit.

1. Deena Moni Radho.

A-d-c's.

1. Sri Lakshmi Chendra Rai Garu.
2. Sri Neela Kanta Rai Garu.

STATE OFFICERS.

Samasthanum Office.

J. Marsh, Esq., M.A. LL.D., Administrator, *on leave*.

Mr. P. Venkannah Pantulu, Dewan.

,, B. Subba Row, Sheristadar.

,, M. Kamaraju Pantulu, Head-accountant.

,, G. Syamalarow Pantulu, E. Head Clerk.

Divisional Officers.

1. Sri Sri Gopinadha Deo Garu, Manager, Jeypore Division.
2. Mr. V. Lingamurti Pantulu, Manager, Gunpur Division.

LAW.

1. Mr. K Somayajulu Pantulu, Vakil.

TALUQ OFFICERS.

Jeypore Division.

1. Sri Jagannadha Qai, Huzur.
2. Bilkari Dass, Koraput.
3. Pithambarasantro, Kotpad.
4. Balabhadra Bakshi Bahadur, Nowrangpur.
5. C. H. Suryanarayana Row Pantulu, Bhyravasingpur.
6. M. Gopalaswami Naidu, Omerkote.
7. K. Seetharamayya Pantulu, Malkangiri.
8. K. Simhagiri Patnaik, Nandapore.
9. M. Hari Kristna Patnaik, Ramagiri.

Gunpur Division.

1. D. Jagannaikulu Pantulu, Gunpur.
2. V. Gangaraju Pantulu, Rayaghada.
3. G. Ramakrishnamma Pantulu, Kalyanasingpur.
4. P. Brahmaji Row Pantulu, Narayanapatam.
5. Gorachendra Santra, Gudari.
6. K. V. Narasimham Pantulu, Madgole.
7. M. Venkannah Pantulu, Narasipuram.

Medical Establishment.

1. M.R.Ry. Vaidyaraj Vinayakamisri Garu.
2. ,, Vikramaraj Payila Garu.
3. ,, Lobiny Maha Patro Garu.

Body-guards Kumandan or Commandant.

1. Mr. Rahim Khan Sahib.

Stables Establishment.

2. Mr. J. Langan, Superintendent

Elephant Establishment.

1. Mr. Pithavasa Mahanti, Superintendent.

Huzur Guards.

1. Sri Krishna Chendra Deo, Commandant.
2. J. Kannayya, Jamadar.
3. D. Hanumantharow, Havildar.

Forest Establishment.

1. Mr. C. A. Eber Hardie, Chief Forest Officer.
2. ,, C. Hammond, Divisional Officer, Jeypore.
3. ,, E. D. Pierce do. Gunpur.

Range Officers.

1. Mr. A. Gordon, Omerkote Range.
2. ,, Barlow, Malkangiri Range.
3. ,, A. M. Clay, Mottu Range.
4. ,, E. G. Burby, Jeypore Range.
5. ,, C. Butler, Rayaghada Range.
6. ,, Samuels, Gunpur Range.

Saw-mills Establishment.

1. Mr. W. A. Aberneithy, Superintendent.

Devasthanum Establishment.

1. D. V. Suryanarayana Row Pantulu, Ameen.

ENGINEERING ESTABLISHMENT,

Overseers.

1. K. Suryanarayana Patnaik.
2. P. Venkatarow Pantulu.

Educational Establishment.

1. V. Bhamiah Chetti, Tutor to Sri Sri Sri Yuwarajah Maharajah.

Thatraz or Commander-in-chief.

1. Sree Narendra Thatraz, Zemindar of Bissam-katak.

Sirdars.

1. Dargi Patro.
2. Lokanadha Jenna.

The Maharajah is of middling stature and of pleasing countenance and his eyes shine forth with remarkable intelligence. He is elegant in deportment and affable and unassuming in his manners. With energies of mind and with splendid talents for business, he is patient, prudent, and attentive to the affairs of the Samastanam and skilful in conducting them. He is conversant with several languages and is a great lover and patron of the arts and the sciences. From what has been said above, it will be easily seen that the Maharajah has been managing the Samastanam with much credit to himself and benefit to his subjects, and towers so high above others that he richly deserves the highest honors that it is in the power of the Government of India to confer on him.

H. H. THE RAJAH OF PALAVANCHA & BHADRACHALAM

(GODAVARI DISTRICT).

Of the most illustrious and well-known family of Palavancha and Bhadrachalam, His Highness Sri Rajah Parthasaradhi Appa Rao Savai Aswa Rao Bahadur, Badshahee Munsubdar and Rajah of Palavancha and Bhadrachalam estates, has all the characteristics of great men, and from his rare perseverance, energy of character and various other virtues, deserves a prominent place in this series.

Bhadrachalam is a taluq and estate in the Godavari District, Madras Presidency, lying between 17° 35′ 45″ and 17° 56′ 30″ N. lat., and 80° 54′ 30″ and 81° 8′ E. long. It contains 315 villages, half of which belongs to an old superior proprietary estate, with 35,656 inhabitants, chiefly Koyas. This taluq with that of Rekapalli, was transferred from the Central Provinces to Madras in 1874. Until 1860 this tract formed part of the Upper Godavari District ceded in that year by H.H. The Nizam. The area with Rekapalli is 911 square miles. Bhadrachalam is the name also of the chief town of the estate. It is about 104 miles from Rajamundry, and 15 from Dummagudem. It receives its name from being near the rock on which Bhadradu performed his devotions. It is celebrated for the temple of Ramachandra who is said to have crossed the river at this spot, on his famous expedition to the island of Ceylon, and also for the annual fair held here in his honour. This temple was built four centuries ago by some Rishis of old but additions have been made from time to time. It

H. H. The Rajah of Palavancha & Bhadrachalam.

Kallikote Estate Press, Rambha.

consists of a main building with a fine dome, flanked by 24 smaller temples on both sides. It is surrounded by a high wall, and may be ascended by steps from near the bank of the Godavari. The sacred jewels are said to be of great value. H. H. The Nizam annually contributes £ 1300 towards the maintenance of the temple. Twenty miles from Bhadrachalam is Parnasala, another shrine of great antiquity. There are also in it court houses, a town school, a jail, a post office, and a police station. About 20,000 people, chiefly from the coast attend the fair held there every April, when English and country cloth, sugar, opium, spices, hardware, &c., change hands to the value of about £ 5000.

The illustrious family from which the Rajah Sahib has sprung dates its origin to a time many centuries ago. One of the most well-known princes of the family in olden days was the recipient of the title of *Aswa Rao* from Maharajah Pratapa Rudra who held sway over Warangal before the Mahomedans conquered Southern India. It would appear that the Maharajah had a horse of the best mettle, and it was ungovernable; but in spite of this defect in the animal, the Maharajah on account of the excellence of the breed conceived a great liking for it. The Prince tried the horse and rode it so well that the Maharajah was agreeably surprised and conferred on him the title of *Aswa Rao* (*aswa* meaning a horse, and *Rao* meaning king). From that time forward the titles has became hereditary.

After the Hindu kingdom of Prataparudra was overthrown by the Mohammadan Emperor of Delhi, the ASWARAOS became independent for sometime. When Tamerlane invaded the country and ascended the throne of Delhi in 1324 A. D., Annappa Aswarao who is now reckoned as the progenitor of the family was the ruling chief of the estate. The Emperor however established his suzerainty over Annappa Aswarao, and granted him a free perpetual sunnud on feudal tenure under the condition of supplying the Imperial army with five hundred soldiers whenever called upon. The Zemindari had been enjoyed by eighteen descendants of the family in succession with independent right free of any kind of assessment. Afterwards the Emperor Aurangzib, also called Alamghir Badsha, once in war sought the help of a chief of this family and a Rajah of Sholapur, and being greatly pleased with the valor and prowess displayed by them both, made them Badshahee Munsubdars.

The ruling Zemindar in 1796 was Rajah Narasimha Aswa Rao. Just then, there were many changes in the Supreme Government at Delhi, and the Zemindar, whose assistance was sought by the Moghul Emperor, asserted his right and refused to comply with his request. Zafraddaulah, also known as Zabid Jung, who was on hostile terms with Rajah Narasimha Aswa Rao foully murdered him and carried away immense treasure, and also the old sunnuds and other important papers connected with the estate. To the titles of the Aswara Rao family were added the distinguished epithets of *Kifuth va avali panâha.* H. H. The Nizam took possession of the estate which under his management was called *Parganai Hasanbad va Senkaragiri Sarkar Kammamet Subai Phirakand Buniyad Hyderabad Deccan.*

After the death of Zafarudowla, Ramachendra Aswa Rao, one of the descendants of Narasimha Aswa Rao, regained his estate and enjoyed it for a year. Later on,

Rajah Venkatarama Narasimha Aswa Rao, the twenty-first in succession from Annappa Aswarao, who originally obtained a sunnud from Tamerlane, was granted a fresh one by Meer Nizam Ali Khan Bahadur in the year 1798, 1240, *Hezree* with the titles of *Rajah, Bahadur, Savai, and Munsubdar*. He was further permitted to maintain an army of two thousand horse, and three thousand foot and carry an *Alam, and Nugâra*, and sunnuds were issued by His Highness the Nizam accordingly. After him, Rajah Narasimha Aswarao, who was commonly known as Sayanna Aswarao, ascended the musnud of Palavancha, and died leaving three minor sons and two daughters; one of the latter died unmarried, while the other was the mother of the subject of this biography. During the minority of these children, the Settipalli family disputed with them for the estate, and the Government having referred the matter to arbitration decided the dispute in favour of the minor princes. The eldest of these princes having died a bachelor, the second one succeeded to the estate and held it for sometime, and was again succeeded by his brother Seeta Ramachendra Savai Aswarao Bahadur, who again obtained a permanent sunnud from the Nizam's Government. But during the reign of this Rajah the estate ran into debt and was mortgaged to a greedy sowcar. About this time, the Nizam made over to the British Government the territory, lying along the left bank of the Godavari, which included a portion of the estate of the Aswaraos called Sri Bhadrachalam. Seetha Ramachendra Savai Aswarao soon after died a bachelor, leaving after him an aged mother, and a married sister. The estate was therefore registered in the name of his mother Ranee Lakshmi Narasamma Rao.

While matters stood thus, the mortgagee sowcar who managed the estate for twelve years instituted a suit for the recovery of a very large amount, the principal having multiplied itself half a dozen times under the most complicated system of compound interest. The defendant Ranee, being unable to contest the suit ably, the sowcar gained his case and obtained a decree for six lakhs of rupees, whereby for only a half of the amount decreed, he carried off the best portion of the estate—the two patties of Mulluru and Ramanujavaram; and had the remaining three lakhs paid out of the Nizam's exchequer. Dispossessed of her ancient estate thus, Ranee Lakshmeenarasamma Rao died in disappointment and despair, leaving a daughter and a daughter's son, Sree Rajah Parthasarathy Appa Rao Savai Aswarao Bahadur in whose veins runs the blood of both Aswarao and Appa Rao families. The young prince smarting under the injustice done to his maternal family, proceeded early in his life to Hyderabad and instituted a suit for the recovery of his maternal estate.

Sri Rajah Parthasaradhi Appa Rao *Savai Aswa Rao Bahadur* is most respectably connected also on the paternal side. He is the eighteenth in descent from the first member of the family, of which Venkayya Appa Rao, generally known as Vijaya Appa Rao, had obtained two sunnuds on the 30th January 1763 from Asaf Jah, whereby he was granted the large Zemindari of Nuzvid, which consisted of eighteen parganas, and was also empowered to keep a *nowbat* and a *jhalardar-pallaki*. To the distinguished titles of *Rajah*, *Bahadur*, *Munsubdar*, *savai*, were added the epithets of *Thahavar-va Jaladat Dastugaha*.

The sixth in succession were Rajah Venkatadri Appa Rao, and his brother, Rajah Narasimha Appa Rao *alias* Narayya Appa Rao. It was about this time that H. H. the Nizam of Hyderabad transferred his suzerainty over the Northern Circars to the British Government. Rajah Narayya Appa Rao had a son, Rajah Venkata Narasimha Appa Rao by his fourth wife, and also two sons Rajah Ramachandra Appa Rao and Narasimha Appa Rao by his fifth wife. The eldest of these, Rajah Venkata Narasimha Appa Rao came to the possession of the eighteen parganas.

In the year 1802 when the British Government commenced the Permanent Settlement of the Zamindaries, Rajah Ramachendra Appa Rao, brother of the said Venkata Narasimha Appa Rao, brought a suit for partition of the estate, and obtained a decree against his brother, whereby the Zemindari was divided into two shares ;, and he obtained the half called the new-Nuzvid Zemindari, and his brother Venkata Narasimha Appa Rao, was given the other portion called the new-Nidadavolu Zemindari. They were also granted *Sunnad-i-Milkhiet Istimerars* for their respective portions.

One unfortunate slip however occurred in this connection. The existence and claims of the other brother of Venkata Narasimha Appa Rao, Rajah Narasimha Appa Rao who was then a minor were not brought to the notice of the Government, and they possibly misunderstood that both Venkata Narasimha Appa Rao, and Narasimha Appa Rao, meant the same person. But on a suit brought by the said Narasimha Appa Rao, the Government found out their mistake, and as they could not alter the decision already passed, they granted him two villages of their own, and 14 villages from the Nidadavolu and Nuzvid Zemindaries. These were called Chevêndra and Tangellamûdy muttas, and permanent sunnuds were also given for the said two muttas. Narashima Appa Rao was succeeded by his son Venkatadri Appa Rao, who died on 18th May 1891, leaving his son and successor, Sree Rajah Parthasaradhi Appa Rao, the present Rajah and Bâdshahee Munsubdar of Palavancha and Bhadrachelam estates. He is as already described the grandson (*Dawhitra*) of Ranee Lakshmi Narasamma Rao, and the British Government recognising his heirship to that Ranee, registered the Bhadrachelam portion of the Palavancha estate in his name in 1869.

Sri Rajah Parthasaradhi Appa Rao Savai Aswa Rao Bahadur was born in 1860 at Ravicherla in the Krishna District. His father was the Rajah of Chevendramuttah, Chanubanda and jageer Ravicherla. At the special request of Rajah Narayya Appa Rao Bahadur of Nidadavole, Rajah Venkatadri Appa Rao Bahadur and the whole family came to Senivarapupeta and settled down there in 1864. A few years after, Rajah Narayya Appa Rao Bahadur died. Both before and long after his death, his brother Sri Rajah Venkatadri Appa Rao Bahadur managed the estate. The deceased Rajah had left behind him two widows, Ranis Papamma Rao and Chinnamma Rao. By virtue of the will left by Rajah Narayya Appa Rao Bahadur to the effect that his moveable and immoveable property should be divided equally between his wives, accordingly they managed the estate jointly. Rani Chinnamma Rad died before Rani Papamma Rao. The latter adopted one of the Rajahs of Nuzvid, Rajah Venkatramayya Appa Rao Bahadur, who died leaving a son, Rajah Narayya Appa Rao Bahadur. Sri Rajah Venkatadri Appa Rao, the father of the subject of this memoir, brought a suit in the Sub-court of Ellore to cancel the adoption made by Rani Papamma Rao Bahadur. The case was decided in favor of the plaintiff. Soon afterwards she adopted Sri Rajah Narayya Appa Rao Bahadur, who was the son of the first adopted Rajah, and who also died some years after adoption. She died a few years ago without adopting anybody. Sri Rajah Parthasaradhi Appa Rao Bahadur as one of the nearest heirs brought about four years ago a suit in the District Court of Rajahmundry for one-third share of the Nidadavole, Baharzalli, Ambarupeta, and Medur estate. The case is pending disposal.

The Nizam's Government under His Highness Meer Mahabuballi Khan Fattezung Bahadur, G. C. S. I., G. C. B., enquired into the case of Rajah Parthasaradhi Appa Rao Bahadur for ten years, and made over the estate to him which had been confiscated by them, on payment of the sum of three lakhs, for which it was so confiscated, with interest at 14 as, per cent. per mensem, amounting to six lakhs of rupees. This order was issued in Fasli 1302 under No. 1032 and 23 Mahesaffur 1311 Hezree 28th Mohar. The Rajah was granted with the estate civil and criminal powers by the Nizam's Government as were formerly enjoyed by his ancestors. He is empowered to sentence offenders to *three years' rigorous imprisonment, to fine up to one thousand rupees, and to award thirty stripes.* He has *unlimited powers* in civil cases, and could try suits for any amount. Besides these powers the Rajah is given permission to keep his own Police, maintain a Registration Department, and issue separate stamps for use in his dominions. The Rajah still claims the remainder of the estate, which the usurious sowcar had managed to obtain.

His Highness the Nizam has the highest respect for the Rajah Sahib, and on every important state occasion he is invited and his *nazar* accepted. He is honored by presents of costly apparel and jewel by His Highness. On the occasion of the installation of the Nizam in 1886, the Rajah's *nazars* were accepted, and he was presented the usual *khillat* (*paga, sallas, a kheenkhabtan,a pair of yellow shawls*) and jewels (a diamond *kalaggee, sarpaish,* a diamond garland, and a pair of diamond *dast bands*). The Rajah Sahib has also the privilege of offering *nazars* in marriage and other important occasions.

The state was owned in the beginning by the MUTYALA FAMILY, and Mutyala Aswa Rao is reckoned as the first of the line of Rajahs that had been enjoying the Zemindari from time to time. The Zemindari was then taken possession of by force, and successively held by the JALAGAM, TANDRA, SETTIPALLI, KANDIMANDLA and DAMARA families. Damara Aswarao adopted a son from KANDIMANDLA FAMILY, and in the dispute between these two families for the Zemindari and the adoption, it was finally settled by the Government by arbitration, that the Zemindari should belong to the DAMARA FAMILY. The last surviving male member of the DAMARA FAMILY died a bachelor leaving his mother and a married sister, and the Zemindari consequently reverted to his aged mother, Ranee Lakshmeenarasamma Rao, the grandmother of Rajah Parthasarathy Appa Rao Bahadur. On the death of the Ranee, Rajah Parthasarathy Appa Rao Bahadur, who is her daughter's son *Dawhitra* became the heir to the Zemindari according to Hindu Law of Inheritance, and has been in possession and enjoyment of the same.

Sri Rajah Narayya Appa Rao Bahadur,
Sri Rajah Venkatramayya Appa Rao Bahadur,
and
H. H the Rajah of Palavancha and Bhadrachalam.

The Rajah Sahib has married one of the daughters of the Rajah of Mylavaram, in the Krishna District and the result of the union is four sons and one daughter, of whom only two are now alive. The elder Sri Rajah Narayya Appa Rao Bahadur has married the second daughter of the Kumara Rajah of Pittapur, and the younger Rajah Venkatramayya Appa Rao Bahadur is a student.

The Rajah Sahib has established a hospital at Buragammala Padu, his present head quarters, and has secured the services of a competent medical officer, and has also employed a vaccinator. The instruments are kept in very good order, and there is an ample supply of good medicines. He has established a Telugu and English school with a good staff of teachers.

The police department is every thing that could be desired under the able supervision of a *Munthazam,* who is a retired officer of much experience having been in the British police for a long time.

The Rajah Sahib has secured the services of an armourer, who was once in the British service and has since retired, and whose work is to keep in good order the muskets belonging to the police, and those of the Rajah Sahib, and also to manufacture such as will be necessary for both.

He has sunk wells for the use of his ryots and has also made new roads. He lately introduced a sugarcane plantation in the Palavancha estate. He has also repaired a number of tanks and wells.

The Rajah Sahib personally disposes of the civil and criminal cases; but when he goes on circuit, his assistants under his orders hear them. The laws in vogue are similar to those observed in British territories.

Whenever the Rajah Sahib proceeds to Hyderabad, His Highness the Nizam's Government receive him with marked respect by furnishing him with a body guard, a state carriage, and an elephant with *amari*.

The Rajah Sahib shortly expects from H. H. the Nizam Subadar powers which his ancestors had exercised and also the *dharmakartha* powers of the Sri Bhadrachalam temple at Bhadrachalam.

From what has been said of the Rajah Sahib it is patent that he is a member of one of the most ancient and well-known families of Southern India. He enjoys the highest titles conferred on his ancestors by the Moghul Emperor, and he is today honored and respected by His Highness the Nizam; but it is to be regretted that the Government of India has not as yet conferred on him any distinction while others who are lower in the social scale have been honored in various ways. By his deeds the Rajah Sahib has proved himself very useful to his ryots and also to the public at large. This is the only Zemindar in Northern Circars who has civil and criminal powers, and whose claims to recognition seem to have been neglected.

Those who know the Rajah Sahib personally, can bear testimony to the fact that he is simple, polite and generous. He is kind to all; he treats the rich and the poor alike. He is very religious but not bigoted. As we have said, he is a member of one of the most ancient families of Southern India holding a permanent sunnud from H. H. the Nizam of Hyderabad, but he has not received one for the Bhadrachalam estate from the British Government, though other Zemindars hold permanent sunnuds in accordance with Regulation 25 of 1802. He is a great lover of justice, and since the time he took possession of the estate, no one could reproach him with a single act of injustice. The high spirited nobleman has done much to ameliorate the condition of his ryots, and moving in the best of societies in Northern Circars and in Hyderabad he has become the great ornament of his court, the prime mover of wise counsels, and the helper of all useful institutions.

H. H. THE RAJAH OF KALLIKOTE AND ATAGADA.

(GANJAM DISTRICT).

All those who have been watching the progress of events from one end of India to the other, can bear testimony to the fact, that there are some Zemindaries to-day in this part of the Presidency, which would seem to confirm the idea, that for any Zemindar who is imbued with honest and noble principles the path to success is an easy one ; and among such Zemindars a chronicler of the history of the Ganjam District is sure to give a prominent place to the Rajah of Kallikote and Atagada. His Highness the Rajah-Sahib Mehrban-i-dostan Sri Rajah Hari Hara Marda Rajah Deo Bahadur is known to the people of the District and those in the Presidency as a nobleman of cultivated mind, of high principles, of polished manners, happy in his family and attentive to the interests of his ryots.

Kallikote is a Zemindari estate in the Ganjam District. It is situated between 19°24′ and 19°48′ N Lat., and between 85°59′ and 85°14′ E Long. The chief town is Kallikote. The estate has an area of 231 square miles and contains 238 villages. The adjoining taluk of Atagada was added to the estate by purchase in 1854 by the former Zemindar. The area of the Atagada estate is 265 squre miles. It contains 203 villages divided into three *muttahs* or sub-divisions. Kallikote lies on the northern boundary of the Madras Presidency, adjoining the Banpur country in Orissa. The soil is generally very fertile, and is well supplied with water.

Sri Hari Hara Marda Rajah Deo Bahadur
Rajah of Kallikote & Atagada.

Kallikote Estate Press, Rambha.

The family to which the Rajah has the honor to belong is a very ancient one. In order to trace its origin we have to go back many centuries. The first member of the family of whom anything is known is Maruva Hari Gopal. The date of his birth and particulars of his parentage are all buried in obscurity but it is said that he belonged to the family of the Rana of Marwar and that he was in the house of Mukund Prasad, the brother of the Rana. Hari Gopal received a very kind treatment at the hands of Mukund Prasad, and in course of time he became a favorite with all the members of the family. He was intimate with them and became fascinated with the beauty of the younger daughter of Mukund Prasad. He told the fact to a Brahmin friend of his, who advised him to banish the idea from his mind, as he should not marry a girl who belonged to another sect, but he added that he would be permitted to do so by secretly performing the penance, known as "Bisbavasu Gandarbhara Rajamantra;" and by giving 5000 gold coins to the officiating priest at Chittore. He accordingly performed the penance for 27 days and on the 28th day, tradition says, a big serpent emerged from the trunk of a huge banyan tree, swallowed him and threw him up again. He lost consciousness for sometime and when he had regained it, the serpent said that it was "Sankanath," that under the orders of the Siva Mahadeva it had given birth to him, that he was its son, that his *gottram* thereafter should be "Nageswara," and that he could marry the younger daughter of Mukund Prasad at Batteswara, near Puri, in the Dekhan. The serpent further added that the grandson of Hari Gopal would become the Rajah of Dekhan. Hari Gopal and the girl Rathna Mani arrived at Puri after a travel of 13 months and 2 days. After

18 years, she gave birth to a son; with him she went to the bank of the Chilka Lake, near the hill called Sammul, where the serpent referred to above appeared unto her. Hari Gopal, having experienced all the vicissitudes of life, was quite tired of them and therefore preferred to become an ascetic. He sold all the valuable jewels he had and with the proceeds he excavated tanks, sank wells, built choultries, and spent the remaining portion of his life in prayers and solitude. He died at the ripe old age of 92. The custom of sati was in existence then and Rathna Mani ascended the funeral pile of her husband. Gopal Ballabha, their son, went to Chittore to perform the funeral rites of his parents as a Brahmin could not be had at Puri to officiate at the ceremony. He met the Brahmin friend of his father and informed him of everything about his parents. He saw his father's maternal uncle, who was pleased to give the young man his grand-daughter in marriage. The married couple with Damodar the son of the Brahmin friend of Hari Gopal and his family and a number of followers, came and settled down at Goppa Kudu, now an island on the Chilka Lake, where they established a temple dedicated to Siva, known as Gupteswara temple. Gopala Ballabha had three sons and a daughter. After some years he went on a pilgrimage when he met Daduva Manasingh, a prominent man of his day, and formed his acquaintance, which soon ripened into friendship, and the result was that Gopal Ballabha gave away his daughter in marriage to the son of Daduva Manasingh. From Chittore he went on a pilgrimage to many places in Northern India, and thence went to Rayapuram in Central India, where he formed the acquaintance of the then Dewan of Hyderabad who had gone to that place. With the Dewan he went to Hyderabad

and paid his respects to the Nizam, who was pleased to give him a sunnud for lands extending to a distance of 400 miles. From Hyderabad he went to Goppa Kudu, where he heard that two of his sons had died. He related all his adventures to the third son Maruva Kali Prasada Rana and died soon afterwards.

Maruva Kali Prasada Rana constituted himself the lord of lands extending through 400 miles as far as the Rushi Kallya river and the Bay of Bengal in the south, and Orissa in the east. Of the 400 miles, 108 miles were forests and 292 miles, arable lands. He became Rajah of half the land and appointed minor Rajahs under him for the rest. The peishcush payable by him to the Nizam, was Rs. 1,400 annually. From the subordinate Rajahs, he received Rs. 48,000 and the income from the estate under his control was 32,000 Rs. He maintained 32 elephants, 150 horses, and 15,000 pikes (sepoys). It was customary in those days to build forts in rocks for perfect safety, and accordingly he built a fort and lived in it. Shortly afterwards his first son died, and his second son went away on pilgrimage without any body's knowledge and after travelling to many places, he went to Oudh, where he saw his brother-in-law, Ramakumar, and married two of his nieces. Maruva Kalli Prasada Rana, who went in search of his son, met him at Benares, while returning with his two wives. They all repaired to their native place. Maruva Kalli Prasada Rana installed his son Kuber Singh as the future ruler and spent the remaining portion of his life in retirement. He left Goppakuda, stopped in Krishnagiri, six miles from Kallikote, and built many temples such as Dadheshwar and Ramachandi. Most unfortunately for him, on a certain day, a cobra was found within the idol of Ramachandi in the temple. He tried to remove it and in the attempt lost his life, as the cobra bit him.

Kubera Mitra had 9 sons, the eldest of them being Durga Prasan. In the battle between the Kings of Bastar and Jaipur, Durga Prasan who went to fight under the orders of the Nizam, distingiushed himself so well that the Nizam conferred on him honors, and loaded him with wealth. While returning, he brought with him some girls of the Chohanu community who were very famous for their beauty and married two of them. One of them poisoned herself and died, while the other died in child-bed. Making his eldest son his successor, he left the place and stopped at Sardhapur a village near Kallikote, where he performed a grand *jagam*. When this ceremony was being performed, there arose a dispute between two of the Brahmins that were present, when the Rajah ordered their immediate removal. In the duel that ensued they killed each other, and the Rajah considering this a bad omen, built two temples in memory of those two Brahmins.

Bholabhadra Rana, the next in succession, went to Oudh, married the eldest daughter of his maternal uncle Harischandra Singh and settled down at Kespur, where he erected a fort. He established 253 villages and dug a canal known as Kharkari which is now the boundary line between Kallikote and Atagada. He performed a *jagam* called "Choyana." He had two sons Narasinga Rana and Deva Ballabba Rana. The former was a great warrior and an accomplished athlête. In a competition between him and one of the warriors of Daduva Durga Mohan Singh, Rajah of Oudh, he came out victor. In another competition with an elephant of the Rajah known as "Bulbul," he showed his prowess and daring by dragging it backwards with its tail, and by pulling it forwards with its tusks. He became famous at Oudh and married the daughter of Rana Beer Singh the brother of the Rajah and stopped there for four years. He had two sons and Chandrasekara, the elder succeeded him. Sudham Chandra Singh and Balaram Sing, brothers of the Rajh of Pattali, went to Puri, where they saw Chandrasekar, took him to their place, and arranged for his wedding with the three daughters of a member of their family. He had eight sons who went to the west for their marriages, when there were evil omens in the State, and the Rajah with a weakness of heart performed a *jagam* called "Chinè" for the well being of his sons. Before the completion of the ceremony two of the Rajah's wives died on one and the same night, while the other died a few days after, in child-bed.

Nilambar Singh, the next in succession, went with his brothers to Maidinapur and married the two daughters of Jalam Singh, a man of great reputation, went to Benares on pilgrimage with his wives and died there. They also jumped into the Ganges and died after the custom known as "Sohayavanam."

The next prominent member of the family was Sarbasewar Deva Rana. He left his native place, went to Puri, formed the acquaintance of the Rajah of that place called Rama Kesari, stopped there for some time, and then married the daughter of the Maharajah of Oudh, Daduva Amrita Singh Takur. There he performed a *jagam* called *Sharada Braja Peya* and died three years after. Raghunatha Deva Rana succeeded him. He married the two daughters of the Maharajah of Puri, and performed a *jagam* known as *Agni Shtom.* Visvambhara Deva Rana, who succeeded him, married the daughter of Rama Kesari, the Rajah of Puri, and also the daughter of Bagala Ameer Singh of Rewa. Then there was a quarrel between the Chohanu and the Rana families. Latchmi Narayana Bhunj of Boudh, Bisva Mohan Singh, Ranjit Singh, and Baneswar Singh of the Punjaub sided the Chohanu people, who were 4000 in number. The quarrel assumed in course of time gigantic proportions and lasted for four years and eight months, many falling victims on both sides. Lakshmi Narayana Bhunj while returning to his place, usurped 120 (coses) of land, now known as Gumsur, which is in the possession of the British Government, while Biswa Mohan, Ranjit, and Banneswar, who came from the Punjaub, took possession of Palur, Biruli and Ganjam respectively. At this stage, there was a dissension between the Rajah of Puri and the Nizam of Hyderabad at Ganjam. In the battle between the two, the Rajah Biswambara who helped the Rajah of Puri lost his life.

The next prominent member of the family was Ramachandra Deo. He ruled over only 45 (coses) of land that were left out of the 400 coses his ancestors had held. With the object of regaining the lost lands, he collected pikes (sepoys), but died before his object was accomplished. Of the 11 others that succeeded him, there is nothing of importance to mention here. Ganga Pershad Rana, who was somewhat prominent, married the daughter of the Maharajah Sivanand Singh of Benares. He died from the effects of a thunderbolt that struck him, leaving behind him his two sons named Gendu and Kirthan.

The brothers who succeeded their father rendered themselves very popular by their amiability and noble nature, and after a time they paid a visit to the Nizam, with the sunnuds their predecessors had received from him. The Nizam gave them a warm reception and granted them lands which were one third of Kallikote, and which is now known as *Chattramutta*. They took arms against Machandri who was in possession of Paluru, defeated him in battle, and while about to kill his wife, she obtained from them a promise that they and their successors, would perform the ceremony known as Pithirni in commemoration of their death. This is performed every year on the first Sunday of the month of *Chaitra*. They secured the Punkala Muttah which is one third of Kallikote, Birudi and Atagada, the neighbouring Zemindaries of Kallikote with a sunnud from the Nizam. Gendu died childless but Kirthan had sons. One of them went to Jalanthra, married the daughter of the Rajah of that place, and stopped there. The other, Syam Sundara Deo, married the two daughters of Ratur Bhibul Singh of Benares. After ruling the estates for a time, he went on a pilgrimage to Rameswaram and other places leaving his son Gangadhar as his successor.

Gangadhar was very religious and therefore established 32 temples in his estates. He extended the canals called Kharkari and Kalajur. He performed a *jagam* at Kontapoda, where he established a *Siva Linga* dedicated to Siddeswar. He went against the Rajah of Puri and defeated him in battle. He was a learned man and he had a host of educated men under him for the management of his estate. He was succeeded by his son Vikrama Deo, who married the two daughters of Ratoor Mahadeo Singh of Benares and also the three daughters of Dadma Aratat Ram Sing. Haricharan Rajah who succeeded him had a chequered career. He was once captured by the Rajah of Parla and kept in confinement for sometime. It was not long, before he married the granddaughter of the Rajah of Parla and got the title of Chotra Sahib. He went with his wife to Kallikote and spent the remaining portion of his life there. He was succeeded by Krishna Saran who performed a *jagam* called *Saradhabaja Peya*. He was ill for a long time, and thinking a change would restore his health, he went to Cuttack, where he died. Balakeswara Deo who succeeded him went with the Rajah of Puri to Cuttack and there they married the daughters of Sri Rama Singh, a member of the Chohanu community. It was on this occasion that the Rajah of Puri conferred on Bala Keswara Deo, the title of *Marda Raja* as a hereditary distinction. The latter discovered the waterfall, known as Nirmala Jhar, where he also built some temples. He dug a big tank Marda Sagar, founded a village and gave it away as a gift to poor Brahmins, and also built a fort called "Mardakote." Jagannadha Marda Raja Deo, who succeeded him, lived to a great age, and had the pleasure of seeing his great grandson.

The next prominent member of the family was Madan Gopal Marda Raja Deo. He had many brothers, and there was a quarrel among them, with the result that some of them were killed, and a few left the place. One of them Nalinakya Marda Raja Deo succeeded him. He founded many villages in his name, and made considerable improvement in the estate.

The people of Ganjam, in a body, at this time, rose against the British Government, when it would appear that the authorities suspecting the Rajahs to have had a hand in it, curtailed their powers, and ranked them among Zemindars.

Jagannadha Marda Raja Deo, who came next was of a religious turn of mind. He spent the major portion of his time at Puri, where he died. Bala Keswara Singh Marda Raja Deo who married the daughter of the Rajah of Surangi, made many additions to the estate. His successor, Narayana Marda Raja Deo, married the first daughter of the Raja of Boudh.

Sri Raja Sahib Mehrban-i-dostan Narayana Marda Raja Deo, the father of the present Rajah, was the next prominent member of the family; he had a brother and a sister; the latter was married to Bhraja Rajah Singh, the Rajah of Dharakota. Sri Narayana Marda Raja Deo was highly accomplished in Sanskrit and Oriya, and in matters military, was an expert. He married the daughter of the Rajah of Boudh. As he was childless by this wife, he married another, the daughter of the Bardana Samanth of Ramapur, a member of the Routh family in Orissa. His third wife was the daughter of Biswanath Singh of Tekkali, a member of the Chohanu community. The second wife had three sons and four daughters, the eldest of them being the present Rajah. The other two sons died and the first of the daughters has married Raja Raghunath Singh of Bali Atagada in Orissa. The second is still unmarried, whilst the third has married the present Rajab of Dharakote in the Ganjam District. By the first wife, Sri Narayana Marda Raja Deo has a daughter, who is the wife of the Rajah of Surangi in the Ganjam District. The building of the temple of Jaganatha, in Kallikote, which was begun seven generations ago, was finished in his time at a cost of over a lakh of Rupees. He built, at a cost of more than 10,000 Rupees a temple at Kallikote, dedicating it to Balinkeswari. He excavated a tank known as Babucha Bandho spending on it 5,000 Rupees. At a cost of about Rs. 25,000, he constructed kitchens attached to the Bhubaneswar temple—one of the famous temples in India near Puri. He purchased a shamiana for Rs. 12,000 and gave it away as a present to the temple in Jagannath. In order that the revenue of a village might be used to meet the expenses of the feeding of the Vaishnavas of Puri, he purchased the village and gave it away as a gift. He established a Sanskrit school for the diffusion of vedic lore. He was a great admirer of ayurvedic medicines, and he encouraged the use of them by securing the services of competent physicians who looked to the medical wants of the people of Kallikote and also those of the surrounding villages. He had under him ten Pundits well versed in Sanskrit. He established two villages in his name and gave them away as gift to poor Brahmins. They are known as "Narayana Puri;" one is in Kallikote and the other, in Atagada. The former is valued at Rs. 20,000, and the latter at 7,000. He once fed 7,000 poor people at Godavari, and gave a gift of a Rupee each; on another occasion he fed 4,000 people at Puri with a gift of Rupee each; once again he fed 4,000 people at Prayagh and gave each of them a Rupee. He performed the *Agnishtom jagam* at Kallikote, spending a lakh of Rupees. The then Zemindar of Atagada failed to pay the peishcush due to Government, and the estate was put to public auction when the Rajah bought it. He built a palace at Kallikote conformably to modern taste and fashion with the necessary appliances and furniture as became a Rajah. He was universally known and respected for his unflagging energy, zeal and charity. He celebrated the marriages of many people at his own cost, and also the *upanayanam* (thread-wearing ceremony) of many poor Brahmin boys. He had on several occasions met the expenses of many poor people who went on pilgrimage. On the occasion of the thread-wearing ceremony of the present Rajah, his father gave away a village as gift to his family priest.

The following letter that was addressed to him by no less a personage than Lord Napier, the then Governor of Madras, speaks for itself, about the Rajah's generosity :—

CHATTERPORE, *July 21st, 1866.*

" SIR, MY FRIEND,

On my arrival in this District, I was much gratified to learn from Mr. Forbes that you had taken a most liberal part in relieving the wants of the people in your estate as well as those who repaired to your residence from the adjoining country. This conduct was most worthy of a person of your high position and descent and inspires the Government with a particular esteem for your character. It is a matter of regret to me that your subsequent illness and the misfortunes which have occurred in your family have rendered it necessary for Government to suspend the measures of relief which you had undertaken. I trust that this period has now passed, and that you will feel yourself justified in co-operating with Government in providing means for the support of the people. Should this be the case it will give me great pleasure to assist you in any way which you may point out to the Collector of the District. If the stores of rice in your possession are exhausted by the number of persons whom you have fed, Government would supply with rice at the cost price at Madras and take upon themselves the charge of transport, or Government would be prepared to exhaust directly a certain share of the expenditure which you may make on the distribution of food. It is very desirable that relief should be afforded at Kallikote or in its immediate vicinity, in order that the people may not crowd to other places where it is difficult to supply the wants of so great a number.

I hope before leaving this country to visit Kallikote and to thank you personally for your charitable exertions.

I remain, Sir,
Your sincere friend and well-wisher,
(Signed) NAPIER,
Governor of Madras.

The Rajah, after a brief illness, died at Kallikote, when he was only 53 years old, leaving behind him three sons and a daughter.

Sri Raja Hari Hara Marda Raja Deo Bahadur, was born at Kallikote, on the 10th July 1872. There was good deal of jubilation all over the estate on hearing the news of the birth of the prince. Many poor were fed in honor of the event, and money was also distributed among them. He was first taught Sanskrit by an experienced pundit of rare attainments. After sometime he was taught English at Kallikote. He did not make much progress, as the death of his father interfered much with his study. The Court of Wards took charge of the the management of the estate and sent the young Rajah to Parlakimedi for education. He remained there for a short time and then went to Madras, where he was placed under the care and tuition of Mr. R. W. Potts, a well-known educationist of his day, who devoted much attention to give the young pupil such instruction in political economy and other kindred subjects as was calculated to enable him to manage his estate well. His intelligence and understanding were seen and admired by those who came in contact with him; his love of pleasure had not so much ascendancy over him as in the case of many other princes of his position. His friends, his teachers, and those who knew him most intimately were thoroughly sensible of the extent of his mental faculties, and when his education came to a close, he was considered as one who had the best chance of gaining a distinguished position among the princes of Southern India. At the completion of his 21st year, in 1883, he took charge of the management of his estate from the Court of Wards, and made his brother *Yuvaraj*.

The Rajah Sahib married in 1894, the first daughter of Babu Brindabhan Chandra Bhunja Deo, Chotra Sahib of Mourbhunj, the paternal uncle of the present Maharajah of Mourbhunj, a Native State in the Balasore District, Orissa. The Rani was suddenly taken ill, when the best of medical aid was obtained but in vain. She died after being confined to her bed only for a short time. The Rajah married his deceased wife's sister in 1895, when under the directions of H. E. the Governor of Madras, the Private Secretary, Mr. MacCartie wrote thus :—

28th May, 1895.

MY DEAR SIR,

I am much obliged for your letter dated 17th instant. I am now to convey H. E. the Governor's congratulations on the successful performance of your marriage ceremonials.

Wishing you a long and prosperous life.

I remain,

Yours sincerely,

(Signed) C. F. MACCARTIE.

It was the Rajah Sahib that purchased the Rambha Estate from Mr. F. J. B. Minchin some years ago. As the major portion of the Chilka Lake which is attached to that estate belongs to the Rajah Sahib we give an account of it from W. W. Hunter's Orissa :—

"A native tradition relates how, about the year of Our Lord 318, a strange race (the Yavanas) came sailing accross the sea, and cast anchor off the holy city of Puri, hoping to capture the temple, with its store of jewels, and treasure-house of costly oblations. But the priests, having for days beforehand seen quantities of litter from the horses and elephants drifting ashore, fled with the precious image and left an empty city to the invaders. The disappointed General Red-arm (Rakhta-Bahu) by name, enraged at the tell-tale tide, advanced in battle array to punish the ocean. The sea receded deceitfully for a couple of miles, and then suddenly surging in upon the presumptons foreigners, swallowed them up. At the same time it flooded a great part of the Puri District, and formed the Chilka Lake.

We take the following from "Wild-life in Canara" by Forbes :—

"The Chilka Lake extends from Pooree to the neighbourhood of the town of Ganjam, a distance of nearly fifty miles, with an average width of ten miles. It is separated from the sea by a narrow sandy plain, but is bordered on its inland side by a varied and beautiful margin of hill and woodland. The lake is fed by a branch of the Mahanuddi (which joins the sea near Pooree), and during the rains its surplus waters cut their way to the sea at the narrowest point of the intervening plain, by a channel which remains open to the tide for the greater part of the year.

"Thus the Chilka is neither wholly salt nor wholly fresh; but it is full of fish, produces immense quantities of prawns, and is in consequence the resort of great numbers of wild fowl. Pelicans and cormorants of different sorts fish its waters, and waders of all sizes and species feed along its shores. The osprey and the fish-hawk are always to be seen there, and vast flocks of wild duck and teal of many varieties make it their favourite haunt.

"Among the rocks at the base of the hills which here and there descend into the lake, colonists of others find a congenial home, and where there is space for a margin of green turf, the peafowl steals out from among the overhanging bamboo clumps, morning and evening, to pick up small marine insects.

"Several islands are scattered about the lake, some flat and rush-grown, where water-rail and teal, and some other species breed, and where collectors of eggs may find specimens not often procurable. But the most remarkable of the group is Bird Island, a high pile of boulders at the southern end of the lake, and distant about two miles from the shore. It is greatly favoured by birds of many sorts as a breeding-place.

"A quarter of a mile from the western shore of the Chilka is Deer Island, a low sandy islet, almost covered with thicket, except along its shores, where the rise and fall of tidal water only permits the growth of a wide margin of saline turf. There are glades here and there among the underwood and yew trees. The whole of the little island is less than a mile. This is the chosen haunt of a small herd of spotted deer which seems to cross at pleasure from the mainland, some of them being almost always to be found on "Deer Island."

"The sandy plain which separates the Chilka Lake from the sea is not more than two miles wide, and it becomes gradually narrower towards the spot where the lake is open to the sea. Considerable herds of antelope graze over this plain, which is in parts thinly clothed with grass, and they may be stalked and coursed there."

The Rajah Sahib is not unknown to the present Viceroy and also to the present and some of the former Governors of Madras. They have all visited the Chilka Lake, enjoyed its beautiful scenery and have spoken in praiseworthy terms of the able management of the estates of the Rajah Sahib. Sir Arthur Havelock wrote thus, under date, 1st April 1898:—

"MY DEAR RAJAH,

I beg your acceptance of the photographs of myself which I am sending you. I take the opportunity of thanking you once more for your kindness and hospitality at Rambha. I retain a pleasant recollection of my visit."

With expressions of regard,

I remain,

Your sincere Friend,

(Signed) A. E. HAVELOCK.

The present Rani is an accomplished lady in Uriya. She has published a book entitled "Balikapato," which is a very interesting reading. The whole of the Ramayana and the Mahabarata is epitomised in it in dialogue form, showing the acute intelligence of the authoress. Besides the Ramayana and the Mahabarata there are also many other points of interest in the book, copies of which are given away gratis. She gave birth to a son in 1898, who died a child of 8 months, when H. E. the Governor of Madras wrote to the Rajah Sahib in the following terms:—

14*th April* 1898.

"MY DEAR RAJAH,

It is with sincere sorrow that I have heard of the terrible loss you have sustained in the death of your little son. I hesitate to intrude upon your great grief, but I should like you to know that I sympathize with you warmly in your sad bereavement.

With sentiments of regard,
I remain,
Your sincere friend,
(Signed) A. E. HAVELOCK."

The Rani Sahiba was safely deliverd of a son in 1899. The prince, pet-named Eric, is in the best of health and spirits, and is placed entirely under the care of a European governess. He lisps English much better than his own language. He has a bright and intelligent look about him. Mrs. F. Harvey Dunn, the governess in charge of the prince, is, though a young lady of great medical experience. She was for about five years a certificated sick nurse and diplômæd midwife in the Government Lying-in-Hospital, and latterly Head

Nurse, General Hospital, Madras. She has been for the last three years a professional nurse under the Rajah Sahib, and mainly in charge of the prince. The arrangement of the furniture in the drawing room at Rambha Palace together with all its decorations has been due to her skill and taste.

The following is a copy of the *sunnud* conferring the personal distinction of *Rajah* on Sri Hari Hara Marda Raja Deo Garu by His Excellency Lord Elgin :—

"To

Sahib Mehrban-i-dostan Sri Hari Hara Marda Raja Deo Garu, Zemindar of Kallikote and Atagada in the District of Ganjam in the Madras Presidency.

I hereby confer upon you the title of *Raja* as a personal distinction.

(Signed) ELGIN,
Viceroy & Governor-General of India."

SIMLA,
The 21st May, 1898.

The Rajah Sahib is the only prince in the whole of the Ganjam District who is quite in touch with the spirit of the times. His mansions, one at Kallikote and the other at Rambha—the most remarkable edifices in the whole of Northern Circars—are completely fitted up with modern appliances. Every possible means has been adopted to establish a veritable air of palatial magnificence. Elaborately carved and brilliantly polished tables, chairs, sofas and various other kinds of furniture supported on guilded frames of exquisite workmanship are placed in the halls and in the rooms. The sleeping apartments are furnished with a degree of splendour and elegance corresponding to the magnificence of the sitting rooms. Standing on the upper storey of the mansion at Rambha,

Mr. A. C. Tatam.

Kallikote Estate Press, Rambha.

one could command a beautiful view of the Chilka Lake, which is 48 miles in length and of a greater portion of the surrounding scenery as well. A number of islands stud the area of waters, and on one of them stands the halting bungalow of the Rajah. The whole of the mansion is provided with gas and electric lights. There is a separate apartment in it for the generation of gas as well as electricity in charge of an electrician who is specially appointed for the purpose. For the quick despatch of business there is a telephonic communication from one portion of the building to another, and there is also a connection from the mansion in Rambha to that in Kallikote, to enable the Rajah Sahib, to pass immediate orders, and also to receive first hand information concerning everything. The mansion in Rambha has got water communication with a basin of water in the compound, and pipes have been laid with connections to almost all the apartments in the mansion.

The three estates are managed by the Rajah Sahib personally, aided by competent assistants. This is the only Rajah at present in Northern Circars who has got a European gentleman as Private Secretary. Mr. Ram Hari Sampat Naick, a member of a highly respectable family, is at the head of the Revenue Department, and Mr. Bholobodro Maha Patro is the Personal Assistant. The latter talks and writes English remarkably well. As both the gentlemen are scrupulously honest the Rajah Sahib has placed implicit confidence in them. Mr. Arthur Cecil Tatam, the Private Secretary, also contributes much to the management of the estate and we must say a few words about him :—

He was born in Woolwich in 1872. His father served

for a number of years in the Horse Artillery, rising to the rank of Captain, got his services transferred to the Remount Department, and stayed for a long time in India. He went to England on sick leave, where he died some years ago, leaving behind him three sons and three daughters. Mr. Arthur Cecil Tatam is second of them. Mr. Edwin Charles Tatam, the eldest of the sons of Captain Tatam, is in England as a private medical practitioner. Captain W. J. Tatam, the third son, is now in Bangalore, attached to the Veterinary Department. He served for two years in South Africa. He passed through the ordeal of the siege of Ladysmith, and was unfortunately one of those that were captured by the opposite side. Mr. A. C. Tatam received his early education in Bedford Modern School, one of the most prominent public schools in England. He then joined the United Services College, Westward Ho, and was there a student for a number of years. He was a great athlete, and was the Captain of the College Cricket Club. He took part in almost all the prominent games and matches, and acquired the name of a champion cricketer of his days. After leaving College, he joined the school of Mr. Windle Taylor of Brampton, Huntingdonshire, and was a tutor for four years. Mr. H. T. Taylor, Collector of the Ganjam District, went to England on leave three years ago, when Mr. Tatam formed his acquaintance. On his returning to India, Mr. Taylor got Mr. Tatam as Private Secretay to the Rajah Sahib. He has been as such for the last two years. He carries on the private correspondence of the Rajah Sahib, arranges for entertainments to European guests, and looks after the stables. He married the daughter of Mr. Richards, retired paymaster of the navy, in July 1901. He is a good huntsman and an intrepid rider. He is a member of the managing committee of the Kallikote College, and a member of the Taluq Board of Ganjam.

The Second Grade College at Berhampore, now known as "Kallikote College" was first established by Government, but some years ago they were going to abolish it; then some of the Zemindars in the District undertook its management. After a few years it was about to collapse for want of proper support when the Rajah Sahib came forward with a liberal donation of a lakh of Rupees, and the institution now stands on a permanent footing.

Till 1897 one of the great wants of the townsmen of Berhampore was a town hall. The Rajah Sahib, who perceived the want, with a generosity becoming a prince, built at his cost a spacious building for the use of the public of Berhampore, and called it "The Diamond Jubilee Hall," in honor of that most auspicious event—the Diamond Jubilee of Her late Majesty Queen Victoria.

The Rajah Sahib has established a free dispensary at Kallikote, the head-quarters of one of his estates, and this has been very useful to the people living there and also to those in the surrounding villages. There is a competent medical officer in charge of the hospital.

The Rajah Sahib has a press of his own called the "Estate Press." Two newspapers in Oriya are printed there; one of them is called *Praja Bhandu*, and the other *Yutkala Maduko*. The former is a weekly paper and the latter, a monthly journal which is printed free of charge to the editor with a view to popularise journalism and enlighten the Oriya speaking community. *Dharma Sastar* is printed and sold at the press at a very cheap rate.

Besides a Sanskrit school, there is also an English school teaching up to the Lower Secondary standard at Kallikote. There are competent teachers attached to both the institutions.

Ten poor Brahmins are fed free every day at Kallikote, and thirty poor of other castes are given rations. *Byragies* who pass Kallikote on pilgrimage are also supplied rations.

The estates are all surrounded by hills, and the forests on them are all systematically and well managed. There are several mines of graphite and manganese. Mr. T. Chaudry, D. D. R., geologist, has been prospecting, and has already discovered some mines of manganese. Every effort is being made to make these mines successful.

There are several places of interest in these estates with grand shrines hoary with age and with views of surpassing beauty. In one of them there is a tank with the idol of Siva in it, whence springs out a fountain of water.

The Rajah Sahib has travelled through India and Upper Burmah. He went twice to Ceylon. He spent his time most usefully in his travels in studying the characteristics of the people.

The revenue from the Kallikote and Atagada estates before the Rajah Sahib took charge of them, was only Rs. 330,000, but now there has been a rapid rise to about Rs. 520,000. The peishcush he has to pay is about 110,000 Rupees. It is to be said to the credit of the Rajah Sahib that he goes out touring to the villages belonging to his estates, hears the complaints of his ryots, redresses their grievances whenever and wherever necessary, and affords them every facility to pay their rent.

One thing that has brought a great deal of honor, the thing which more than any other raises him in the estimation of the paramount power is that in his estate men of malpractices, loose behaviour, corruption and bribery have been rooted out, as the Rajah Sahib himself takes a keen interest in all departments of business. By all who have had any dealings with him, his character is readily seen and admired, and they have expressed it as their opinion, that it is impossible to overlook his indomitable energy, clear intellect, sound judgment, and sterling integrity, as well as that earnestness of purpose which is indispensable to greatness.

As regards irrigation works, the Rajah Sahib is in no way backward; many tanks have been restored completely, and many new ones have been formed. He has spared neither pains nor money in constructing new irrigation works wherever practicable.

The Rajah Sahib is an excellent horseman; he can remain a number of hours on the saddle without showing any signs of fatigue. His love for horses amounts to a passion, and he maintains a good stud for his personal use. He has carriages of almost all descriptions of up-to-date model of English make.

Most of the leisure hours of the Rajah Sahib are spent in intellectual improvement; he has gained a wide acquaintance with general literature and has become acquainted with such topics as go to form a well-trained mind. By preference he gives his attention to political, constitutional, industrial, and social history, and has acquired all the knowledge that the books at his command could give regarding the present condition of the leading nations of the world. Besides all this, the Rajah Sahib is deeply imbued with noble principles; he has always been a firm friend of popular freedom, and has earned an honorable reputation as the patron of those movements that are calculated to do good to the public at large and as the helper of the suffering and the deserving. To be one of the chosen men of the people and most respected encouragers of young India, and the generous host and princely entertainer of viceroys and governors indicates a nature of wonderful breadth of mind and nobility of sentiment.

As an illustration of the broad nature of the Rajah Sahib's sympathy, it may be interesting to note that in addition to the numerous educational institutions, to which he has given his support, he has more or less actively identified himself with many charitable institutions. Every lineament of his face appears to bespeak generosity of heart, rectitude of principle, and innocence of soul. He is not influenced by the narrow and jaundiced views of superstition and bigotry. The advantages of education and high principles have rendered him the friend of his district, the pride of his race and the glory of his age. It is a great pity that a prince of such brilliant qualifications, one who has proved himself by his deeds and advanced ideas that he is above the average run of the princes of Southern India, has not yet received any due recognition of his merits. If the Government of India be pleased to confer the title of 'Maharajah' and the honor of a knighthood on him, such a distinction will be but a just reward for the eminent services he has rendered both to his subjects and to the public at large.

Sri Rajah V. Veerabhadra Raju Bahadur Garu in uniform.

Kallikote Estate Press, Rambha.

SRI RAJAH VAIRICHERLA VEERABHADRA RAJU BAHADUR GARU, ZEMINDAR OF KURUPUM

(*VIZAGAPATAM DISTRICT*).

Endowed with those splendid talents and energy that characterize the representatives of aristocracy, the Zemindar of Kurupam, Sri Rajah V. Veerabhadra Raju Bahadur Garu, possesses all the private and domestic virtues, and from the careful training he received when young, and from the ability and skill he has already displayed in the conduct of business, merits a prominent place in the modern history of Southern India.

The Kurupam Zemindari is situated in the north-eastern part of the Vizagapatam district, and lies partly in the jurisdiction of the Deputy Tahsildar of Parvatipur, and partly in that of the Gunupur Deputy Tahsildar, in the division of the Senior Assistant Collector of Parvatipur. Its area is nearly 700 square miles, of which about 450 square miles are agency tracts, and 250 square miles are plains. The total number of villages in the Kurupam Zemindari (including the lately purchased estate of Chemudu) is 274, of which about 200 are agency villages, while the rest are situated in the plains.

The area of the forests belonging to the estate is not less than 400 square miles. The country, being situated partly in the agency tracts and partly in the plains, presents a beautiful variety of hills and dales interspersed with extensive plains and cultivated lands. The forests of the estate contain excellent timber, and abundant game of all kinds.

The total revenue of the estate from all sources is over a lakh of rupees annually, and the revenue of the agency villages is capable of great development, while if some irrigation projects which are now under contemplation, are carried out, the revenue of the villages situated in the plains promises to rise considerably. The Peishcush payable to the Government by the Kurupam Zemindari, including the estate of Chemudu, is Rs. 18,987-14 annas, while the land cess is Rs. 5,173-9-4.

About the origin of the Kurupam Zemindari, Mr. Carmichael's Vizagapatam District Manual says as follows :—

" The Kurupam Zemindari (with the exception of the Gumma Hunda which was added by the favour of Gopinath Deo of Parlakimidi about the middle of the 18th century) was granted to Sanyasi Raju, afterwards honored with the title of *Vairicherla* which has the same meaning as *Satrucherla*, by Visvambhara Deo of Jeypore;" while the Report of the Committee of Circuit in Vizagapatam, and Chicacole Districts, dated 12th September, 1784, says as follows :—

" Kurupam, the most northern part of the Vijayanagaram Zemindari was formerly dependent on the Nandapuram (Jeypore) Rajah, and held by the family of Dimalash, paying a tribute of seven thousand rupees, besides having 2,000 men in readiness for the superior Rajah's service. It remained in the same family till 1773, when Seetharamaraju (of Vijayanagaram), being at an entertainment there, took it by surprise, secured all its wealth and made the Rajah and his relations prisoners.

"The inhabitants resenting this breach of hospitality were continually in arms, and besides destroying the crops put him to great expense in supporting troops, and in presents to appease their principal leaders. On using his influence, Vijayaramaraju restored the country to Siva Ramaraju, the dispossessed Rajah, who was to pay him Rs. 40,000."

Of the political status of the Zemindars in the Northern Circars in general, Dr. MaClean's Presidency Administration Manual says: "The Rajahs in the Northern Circars were at first treated as Feudatories, and paid tribute, being expected in return to keep the hill tribes in order. In 1802, however, a permanent settlement was introduced and the chiefs became Zemindars, retaining the management of the land revenue of their estates, but being themselves handed over to the judicial power. In Vizagapatam, there are 14 Zemindaries, all of ancient lineage, &c.

"Of these 14 ancient Zemindaries in the Vizagapatam District, Bobbili, Vijayanagaram, and one or two extinct Zemindaries, are situated in the plains while the rest are Hill Zemindaries the largest and the most important of which is Jeypore and next in rank, extent and importance are Kurupam, Madogole, and one or two more."

Of the origin and political status of the Hill Zemindaries, Mr. Beaufoy, in his report on the Northern Circars in 1792, writes as follows :—

"The Zemindars who inhabit the several districts that constitute the Northern Circars may be considered as composed of two different classes.

"(1) Those who reside in the hills on the Western frontier, (2) those whose principal possessions are in the plains, between the highlands and the sea.

"The former, the Hill Zemindars, secure in the woody and unwholesome heights they inhabit, and encouraged by the hope of an eventual asylum in the dominions of the Nizam or the Rajah of Berar, are rather tributary Princes than Subjects, and often furnish examples of successful depredation or unfinished revolt.

"Surrounded like the chieftains of the Feudal times by Military tenants, whose lands are held on under stipulations of personal service (Kurupam Zemindari contains 17 villages of this class), and whose ardour is often increased by the bond of family attachment and the strong enthusiasm of clanship, they are always prepared for the excursions of predatory war.

"Of humbler lineage than the chieftains of the hills, the greatest of the lowland Zemindars are descended from those officers and revenue agents of the Sovereigns of Orissa, who were employed by the Mussulman conquerors in the management of their new acquisitions, and in the collection of taxes they imposed. Hence they are considered by the inhabitants of the hills as traitors to their ancient lords, and usurpers of their rights.

"Of such Hill Zemindaries situated in the Vizagapatam District, Jeypore, as stated above, is the first, and next comes Kurupam."

The family records go to prove, and it is also traditionally believed that the Kurupam Zemindari was obtained by one Vairicherla Agniveerudu in recognition of his valour and military service rendered to some chief. The name Agniveerudu is very significant, meaning "fiery valour." Vairicherla has become a surname and is adopted by his descendants. Nothing is known of about five or six generations subsequent to Agniveerudu, and the name on record after him is Vairicherla Pedda Sanyasiraju. From historical accounts, we understand that Sivarama Raju, the son of Pedda Sanyasi Raju, was the contemporary of Seetharam Raju of Vizianagram, and we can therefore safely say that the origin of the Zemindari was about the middle of the 15th century.

The next in line of succession after Vairicherla Pedda Sanyasiraju was his son Vairicherla Sivarama Raju, who succeeded to the estate with good credentials as he was Dewan to his father. We take the following about Sivarama Raju from Mr. Carmichael's Vizagapatam District Manual :—

"Sivarama Raju of Kurapam joined heartily in the rebellion against the Pusapaties, which broke out about the period of the establishment of the first chief in council, and when the Company's troops under Captain Mathews advanced into Jeypore in the year 1774, he attacked the rearguard and cut off their supplies. On their return from Jeypore, the Pusapaties led Captain Mathews to Kurapam and arrested Siva Rama Raju with all his family. The Zemindari was restored to the old family by the Collector of the Northern Division in 1706, and the pe manent settlement of 1802 was made with Sivarama Raju's son Chinna Sanyasiraju."

Chinna Sanyasiraju was the first to rule the estate under the Permanent Revenue Settlement for a period of 28 years, from 1802 to 1830. He instituted many salutary reforms, established agraharams, and dug tanks. As he was without a heir he adopted Sitharama Raju, a son of his cousin, duly intimating the fact to the authorities concerned. Sitharama Raju was as good as his adoptive father, and there was considerable improvement in the estate during his time. He died in 1830 leaving behind him an only infant who survived his father but for a few days. Virtually his widow, Subhadramma Garu, succeeded to the estate, and ruled it for eleven years, from 1830 to 1841. She endeared herself to the hearts of everybody; her piety and charitable nature are still remembered by many an old man and woman. As she had no issue, she adopted her grandson, Sree Suryanarayana Raju Bahadur Garu, the father of the present Zemindar.

It is clear that the chiefs of Kurupam were very influential, and played an important part in the history of those parts of India when the government of the country was unsettled, when native princes and chiefs were partly brought under British yoke and partly resented it, when plotting and rebellion were the common occurrences of the day, and when the country was torn asunder by dissensions. Long before the advent of the British, the chiefs were very powerful, and were dreaded abroad for their ferocity, as it was common with them to make inroads upon villages, and make them their property by dint of sword, arrows, and bow-strings, in the use of which they were well skilled. Thus in addition to the property they had inherited from their ancestors, they had acquired forts and new estates comprising many villages, and constructed temporary mud forts with bamboo fencing so as to prevent the coming in of arrows which were the common weapons of the day. Among the forts acquired in this way by the chiefs of Kurupam, may be mentioned those of Gummakota, Viswanathapur, Tadikonda and Kumbi Kota. They would go to these places, subdue them, make them their own, settle for a time there until all fear of rebellion from the subjugated has vanished, and then proceed on their march of depredation to another convenient quarter. It will also be interesting to note in this connection that in the Thatikonda valley is constructed a fort of this kind, in which are located a number of entire villages. This was to prevent the coming in of arrows upon those thatched roofs. It was the custom in those days for robbers to append a firebrand or a burning torch to an arrow, and let it go on these thatched roofs so that they might take fire, and the inmates of the houses might come out affording the free booters facilities for carrying on their work.

We have ample proof on record that these influential chiefs were engaged in intrigue and warfare about 1774, the time of Warren Hastings, the first Governor-General of India. These powerful princes (then called Deos) such as Jeypore, and chiefs under them such as Kurupam and Madugole, were, with ample privileges, after the Permanent Settlement of 1802, styled by the common designation of Zemindars.

Sri Rajah Suryanarayana Raju Bahadur Garu was a child of three years when his adoptive mother died, and hence the estate was taken under the Court of Wards. It was in 1857 that the Rajah Sahib was put in charge of the estate with a large cash balance. During the 34 years of his rule, the estate witnessed numerous changes for the better. His statesmanship was admitted by every one of the officers who came in contact with him. He dug a number of tanks, cleared up numerous jungle tracts, and brought many waste lands under the plough. It is gratifying to observe that the revenue of the estate tripled itself in his time. He married Sri Sowbhagyavathi Patta Mahadevi Garu and the fruit of their union is the noble subject of this memoir.

He purchased the Zemindari of Chemudu, and also several agraharam villages and inam lands, besides investing a large sum of money on the mortgaging of many neighbouring agraharams and mokasas. He has immortalized his name by establishing a new town called "Suryanarayana Raju Puram." He was very religious all through his life. He built two temples, one dedicated to Siva, and the other to Vishnu, with an endowment of lands for their upkeep. In spite of his numerous charities, there was found in his treasury, after his demise, a cash balance of a large sum of money.

When we review his life, we cannot but admire in him the great qualities which distinguished him throughout his long and successful career and made him one of the greatest men of his race. He died in January 1891, leaving behind him many friends and relations to bemoan his loss, and carrying with him the good will of his subjects.

Sri Raja Veerabhadra Raju Bahadur Garu was born on the 6th September 1877. As the only male child of the Vairicherla family he was the pet of his parents and of everybody else connected with him. While a boy, his precocious intelligence and quiet habits were admired by all. His father was mindful of his duty towards the bringing up of his son, both on English

Sri Rajah V. Veerabhadra Raju Bahadur, Garu in native costume.

Kallikote Estate Press, Rambha.

SRI RAJAH VASUDEVA RAJAMANI RAJA DEO GARU, ZEMINDAR OF MANDASA

(*GANJAM DISTRICT*).

Mandasa is one of the most ancient zemindaries in the Ganjam District, and the chief members thereof in olden days distinguished themselves in many a battle-field, and hence it claims to be the possession of a noble family of historical importance. The present Zemindar Sahib Mehrban-i-dostan Sri Rajah Vasudeva Rajamani Raja Deo Garu, a highly enlightened prince with broad views and noble generosity has rendered himself very popular with all, and has won golden opinions from collectors and governors.

The first member of the family to which the Zemindar has the honor to belong was a famous Kshatrya named Varma Simha of the lunar race who came to prominence in the 13th century. The estate obtained by him has been during all these centuries in the enjoyment of the family in unbroken perpetuity. Sri Srinivasa Rajamani Raja Deo, the grandfather of the present Rajah, had a splendid record for great ability and noble character. He was very charitable ; temples, agraharams and other institutions of public utility that he established are ample evidences of his large-heartedness. The choultry built by him at Haripur has been of much use to the pilgrims that go to Benares and Rameswaram. As he was a nobleman of high respect and vast experience, he was accepted as a safe counsellor by almost all the officers who came in contact with him ; he was frequently consulted by them in matters of importance. He was specially of great service to the collectors of the district. Whenever a disturbance took place he was the first to render all possible aid to suppress it and to restore peace and order by sending his own armed men and retainers. The Government of Madras had reposed so much confidence in him, that he was generally commissioned to capture on their behalf the rebels and mutineers. On a certain occasion, there were within the jurisdiction of another Zemindar in the District, insurrections and rebellions and everything was in confusion and disorder. All this called for the interference of the Government of Madras, but they did not disturb the management of the estate by the Zemindar, because of the surety of the Rajah of Mandasa in whom they had placed implicit confidence and for whom they had the highest respect.

Rajah Sri Jagannadha Rajamani Raja Deo Garu, C.I.E., the father of the present Rajah, was a scholar, artist, and statesman. His loyalty to the British throne which he had inherited from his ancestors, was of a superior order, and the successful manner in which he had managed the estate was admitted on all hands. He was the recipient of the following sunnud in 1877, conferring on him the title of Companion of the Indian Empire :—

" *Victoria by the Grace of God of the United Kingdom of Great Britain and Ireland, Queen, Defender of the Faith, Empress of India, Sovereign of the Order of the Indian Empire.*

To

SRI RAJAMANI RAJA DEO,

ZEMINDAR OF MANDASA,

MADRAS.

GREETING :

Whereas We are desirous of conferring upon you such a mark of Our Royal favour as will evince the esteem in which we hold your person and the services which you have rendered to Our Indian Empire, We have thought fit to nominate and appoint you to be a member of Our said Order of the Indian Empire, We do by Grant of the Dignity of a Companion of the Order of the Indian Empire, to Sri Rajamani Raja Deo of Mandasa, these presents grant unto you the dignity of a Companion of Our said Order and hereby authorize you to have, hold and enjoy the said dignity and rank of a Companion of Our said Order, together with all the singular privileges thereunto belonging or appertaining.

"Given at Our Court at Osborne, under Our Sign Manual and the Seal of Our said Order, this first day of January, 1878, in the Forty-first Year of Our Reign."

By the Sovereign's Command,
(Signed) SALISBURY."

In further appreciation of the Rajah's excellent management of the estate he was authorised to keep two pieces of cannon by the grant of the following license :—

No. 49.

GOVERMENT OF INDIA,
HOME DEPARTMENT.
PUBLIC,
SIMLA, *the 22nd August* 1887.

LICENSE.

With reference to rule 12 of the rules made by the Governor-General in Council under the Indian Arms Act, 1878, and published in the notification of this department, No. 518, dated the 6th March 1879, the Zemindar of Mandasa in the Ganjam District of the Madras Presidency is hereby licensed to possess two cannon.

By Order of His Excellency
The Viceroy and Governor-General,
(Signed) A. P. MACDONNELL,
Secretary to the Govt. of India.

The title of *Rajah* as a personal distinction was conferred on him by the Government of India in 1887, when H. E. the then Governor of Madras, wrote as follows :—

MADRAS, *January* 6*th*, 1886.

" MY FRIEND,

Now at last I am able to address you as *Rajah* officially and I need hardly say that it gives me very great pleasure to do so.

Long may you live to enjoy honors and to benefit your people on your noble estate.

Believe me to be,
Your sincere friend,
(Signed) M. E. GRANT-DUFF."

The Rajah Sahib and Sir M. E. Grant-Duff were on very friendly terms, and they always corresponded with each other. We give here one of the letters written by his Excellency to the Rajah Sahib :—

November 6*th*, 1886,
GUINDY.

" MY DEAR RAJAH,

It is always a great pleasure to me to hear from you and I trust that when I am in Europe I may now and then have tidings of your welfare.

I think it must be you who have sent me a very pretty little carved bottle which came yesterday from Mandasa with a letter.

Will you permit me to offer two books of myself—the one published and relating to my life here—the other privately printed and belonging to my pre-Indian life.

" I should feel it a great honor to be thus represented in your ancient castle where you so kindly received me.

I am,
With every good wish,
Your most sincere friend,
(Signed) M. E. GRANT-DUFF."

As specimens of local art and handicraft, the Rajah sent some beautifully carved boxes to the Colonial and Industrial Exhibition held in London, of which His Most Gracious Majesty King Emperor (then Prince of Wales) was President. The Rajah was the recipient of two medals for the carved boxes. Much credit is due to him for being the first to establish an English school in the District. Mr. G. S. Forbes congratulating him on the interest he evinced in matters relating to education wrote in the following terms:—

" MY DEAR RAJAH.

* * * * *

I wish all the Zemindars would follow your excellent and generous example in the establishment of schools. I hope your are going on satisfactorily and that all the villages on your estate are taking advantage of them."

In honor of the visit of His Royal Highness, the then Prince of Wales to India, the Rajah endowed a scholarship called " The Prince of Wales' Scholarship."

Sir M. E. Grant-Duff, in a public speech made at Bezwada, classed the Rajah of Mandasa with the Maharajah of Vizianagram, and the Rajahs of Bobbili and Pittapur and said: " We have in these north-eastern Districts, men who, like the Maharajah of Vizianagram, the Zemindars of Mandasa and of Bobbili, are doing much in various ways for the enlightenment of those around them."

In recognition of the public spirit and loyalty of the Rajah, the Government of Madras in 1877 granted to him the following certificate :—

"By Command of His Excellency the Viceroy and Governor-General this certificate is presented in the name of Her Most Gracious Majesty Victoria, Empress of India, to Sri Rajamani Raja Deo Garu, Zemindar of Mandasa, son of Sri Srinivasa Rajamani Raja Deo Garu, in recognition of his services to the State in handing over free of cost the land required for a road through his Zemindari and of the public spirit and loyalty which he has evinced in various ways,"

Sri Rajah Vasudeva Rajamani Raja Deo Garu, the eldest of the three sons, was placed, while young, under the careful supervision of his father; and under the instructions of his teachers he learnt English, Telugu, Bengali and Urdu. The Rajah Sahib wishing to show his loyalty to the British Government volunteered himself to place his services at the disposal of the Government of Madras and to proceed to South Africa at a time when the Boer war assumed gigantic dimensions and threatened to become a serious matter. This was just before the relief of Ladysmith when Field-Marshal Lord Roberts was of opinion that every available man in the Empire would be required for active service in the war. The Rajah spared no time in making arrangements about the management of the estate by the Government of Madras during his absence in field service. On hearing that Ladysmith had been relieved, and that there was no necessity for him to join the war service, the Rajah rescinded the arrangements he had made. At every successful stage of the war there were great rejoicings at Mandasa and prayers and thanksgivings in the temple.

On hearing the death of Her Most Gracious Majesty, the Queen-Empress Victoria, the Rajah evinced his sympathy in various ways. To commemorate the memory of that august lady, he came forward to build a hospital last year and the foundation stone was laid by the Collector of the district. The building is in course of construction and it will soon be an accomplished fact. He maintains a bed in the Gosha Hospital, and has endowed a secondbed. To the Victoria Memorial Fund, the Dowager Ranee and the Ranee of Mandasa subscribed Rs. 2,000. The following letter was addressed by H. E. Lord Ampthill, on the 3rd October 1901 to the Rajah Sahib :—

"To

THE ZEMINDAR OF MANDASA.

DEAR SIR,

I wish in reply to your letter of the 26th September last, to thank you most sincerely for the generosity with which your family has come forward, to support the Women's Victoria Memorial Fund. Will you be so good as to express my gratitude to the Dowager Ranee, and to your lady the Ranee of Mandasa.

Believe me,

Yours very truly,

(Signed) AMPTHILL."

The Rajah Sahib takes much interest in students' hostels, and the present additional ward to the students' hostel at Berhampore owes its existence to his generosity.

When the Rajah Sahib heard of the redemption of the Victoria Town Hall at Madras, he not only subscribed Rs. 3,000 towards it but also induced many of his friends to contribute towards the movement. He maintains a lower secondary school, a girls' school, a sanskrit school, and a primary school for boys. He has instituted a scholarship for students that study for the B. A. Degree Examination in the Vizianagram College after passing the F. A. Examination from the Parlakimedi College or the Kallikote College.

In 1897 the Government of India granted the following certificate to the Rajah Sahib in recognition of his services as a member of the District Board of Ganjam and also for the special interest taken by him in vaccination :—

"By command of His Excellency the Viceroy and Governor-General in Council, this certificate is presented in the name of Her Most Gracious Majesty Queen Victoria, Empress of India, to Sahib-i-Mehrban-i-dostan, Sri Vasudeva Rajamani Raja Deo Garu, Zemindar of Mandasa, son of Sri Jagannatha Rajamani Raja Deo, in recognition of his services as a member of the District Board of Ganjam and of the special interest taken by him in vaccination."

The Rajah Sahib manages the affairs of the Samasthanam assisted by his brother who is known as Thatraz (Commander-in-chief), and also by the Dewan, Mr. Chalapathi Sastri Garu, a gentleman of great worth and excellent principles.

It is gratifying to note that the Rajah Sahib is very kind to all his ryots, and whenever they represent to him their grievances, he gives them a patient hearing and affords them ready redress. His qualities both of head and heart are admired by everybody; he is a perfect gentleman; he is very charitable and sympathetic to the poor; his loyalty to the British throne is exemplary; and he has been maintaining the prestige and honor of his family by his generous acts and noble behaviour.

Rai Bahadur K. Jagannadha Chettiar.
Sri Rajah Jagavira Rama Ettapa Nayaker Bahadur.

Kallikote Estate Press, Rambha.

SRI RAJAH JAGAVIRA RAMA VENKATESWARA ETTAPPA NAYAKAR BAHADUR, ZEMINDAR OF ETAIYAPURAM

(*TINNEVELLY DISTRICT*).

The Zemindar of Etaiyapuram, who belongs to the ancient stock of a Hindu family that furnished to the country warriors and statesmen, has inherited all the noble and generous qualities that characterised his ancestors, and is now in the highest estimation of the Government of Madras; and, as his sentiments are guided by justice and moderation, he is most loved by his ryots.

The ancient Zemindari of Ettayapuram consists at present of Ettayapuram proper, Nagalapuram, Golwarpati, part of Elayarampannai, and Sundarapachayapuram, in the Tinnevelly District, and Vallanadhi Division of the Gandamanaickanoor Zemindari in the Madura District, purchased by the Court of Wards in 1896.

The total area of the Zemindari is 647 square miles or 415,428 acres approximately; of this extent, the cultivable area is 374,441 acres, and the rest consists of waste lands, and hill and forest tracts.

The nature of the soil is rich black cotton interspersed with red loam here and there. The approximate annual revenue is 415,000 Rs. and the annual Peishcush is Rs. 135,000 The chief crops are cotton, cumbu, and cholam, Out of 60 lakhs worth of cotton annually grown in the Tinnevelly District, 30 lakhs worth is grown in the Zemindari.

The hill and forest tracts are game preserves. The greatest and most important of them is the Kurumalai reserve, nearly 3 miles east of the Kumarapuram station of the South Indian Railway. The game preserved consists of deer, antelope, hare, and wild boar. They are preserved chiefly with a view to afford sports to gentlemen visitors, majority of whom are European Officers of rank in the service of His Majesty's Government. The South Indian Railway skirts the Zemindari. The nearest Railway station is Koilpati which is nine miles west of Ettayapuram and which is connected with it by a metalled road.

Tradition says, and there are also records to show, that the ancestors of the Zemindar of Etaiyapuram were at Chandragiri, being in possession of territories adjacent to it. The first of those prominent among them was Periappa Nayakar who flourished in 856 A. D. Nine generations passed away without any member in the family doing anything worthy of record.

The tenth in succession was Nallama Nayakar, who was distinguished for his prowess and adventurous career. He had a great desire to proceed to Vijianagram, which was then in the height of its glory and to pay a visit to the Rajah, but one thing that stood in his way before venturing to pass the gates of the fort to interview the Rajah was that he should choose one of the two alternatives—either he should wrestle with a powerful man, named Soman, and overcome him, or pass underneath the gold chain that Soman had attached to his left leg. Nallama Nayakar whose body was of a colossal build chose the former alternative, and in the combat he came off victorious, and beheaded Soman. The eight brothers of the gate-keeper threw themselves on the mercy of Nallama Nayakar and sought his protection. He fixed the head of Soman to a spear, and his garments stained with blood to the point of a lance, and with these things presented himself before the King, who, admiring the valour of Nallama Nayakar welcomed him to his court, and presented him with a gold head to be worn as a badge on his left leg, and allowed him to use the blood-stained cloth as a banneret. To commemorate the fact of his having spared the lives of the eight brothers of Soman, the King conferred on Nallama Nayakar the title of *Ettappan* (meaning father of eight), and also presented him with two state fans, besides lands and villages. By the special order of the King, Nallama Nayakar was taken round in procession before he left the place. From that time forward the appellation "Ettapan" has been used by all the successive Zemindars of Etaiyapuram. The gold head, on the occasion of the installation ceremony, is tied to the left leg of the installed Zemindar by the descendants of Soman referred to above, and the blood-stained banneret is also carried.

Kumara Muttu Ettappa Nayakar, the fourteenth in descent, migrated to Madura with a number of his kinsmen owing to disturbances and insurrections by Mahomed Alaudin, and paid his respects to Adi Vira Parakrama Pandian, the Rajah of Madura, who, on hearing the antecedents and noble ancestry of Kumara Muttu Ettappa Nayakar granted him and also his followers extensive lands and villages, such as Anaiyur and Karukotanpatti, and they settled down there. Kumara Muttu Ettappa Nayakar brought order out of the chaos then existent and engaged himself in useful pursuits. As he had no issue for a long time he built a temple and dedicated it to (Kumara) Subramaniaswami. Shortly after this, he was blessed with a son, who was named Kumara Ettappa

Nayakar. It was this gentleman that put down the pride of an outlaw named Muvarayan and ultimately put him to death levelling his fort to the ground. In recognition of the valorous deed of Kumara Ettappa Nayakar, the Pandian king conferred on him the title of "Sundara Pandya". As Sundara Pandya Ettappa Nayakar had acquired a wide reputation for his enterprising spirit and daring valour, the Pandian king empowered him to quell disturbances in the south, and to restore order and peace as every thing was in confusion and disorder by marauders and upstarts. He accordingly proceeded to Satur, built a fort, and left one of his kinsmen, Nallama Nayakar, in charge of it, which thereafter came to be known as "Nallama Nayakar Kottai"; there still remain some ruins of the fort to the east of Satur and on the south banks of the river.

The next prominent member of the family, Kumara Ettappa Nayakar, brought the Maravars of Elambunom to subjection, and granted the privilege of carrying his, and his successors' palanquin on two of them, Arjuna Thalaven and Muttirala Thalaven and their descendants. He won the esteem and regard of one of the viceroys of the Pandyan king, by name Jagavirarama Pandyan, by collecting the taxes that remained unpaid by the Marawars of Elambunom, which were 50 bullock loads of money. The viceroy being pleased with the integrity and unflinching energy that characterised Kumara Ettappa Nayakar, made him a grant of Elambunom, Peddharajapuram, now known as Peddapuram, Pandavamangalam, Suraikapati, Eeral, Valampati, Ramanuttur, and Naduvirapatti, yielding a revenue of Rupees 19,250. He went a step further in his munificence by making the

Nayakar the warden of Tiruchuli, conferring on him the title of "Jagavirarama," and by giving him the village of Padavathapully for his palanquin expenses. He continued lord at Elambunom for more than a quarter of a century.

Jagavira Rama Ketchila Ettappa Nayakar, the 19th in succession, subdued Saya Malai and added 15 surrounding villages to it. He was made guardian of one of the 72 bastions of Madura.

Jagavira Rama Kumara Ettappa Nayakar, who was the next Zemindar, has the credit of having built the present town of Etaiyapuram in January 1567, and also the Siva temple there. The King of Madura, Kumara Krishnappa Nayakar, and the Zemindar of Etaiyapuram, proceeded to Travancore and attacked the fort of Eraneel. While returning, the latter was treacherously killed by an arrow discharged by a concealed foe. The former being overwhelmed with grief on account of the sudden death of his comrade made to the family of the deceased a grant of Calugumalai, and also affixed the word "Aiyan" to the names of the succeeding members of the family.

The next prominent member was Jagavira Rama Ettappa Nayakar Aiyan, who went with the King of Madura, Muthu Krishnappa Nayakar, to collect certain dues owing to him in Travancore. Sri Vanji Marthanda, the then Rajah of Travancore, received them very kindly and rendered them every possible aid.

Jagavira Rama Ketchila Ettappa Nayakar Aiyan, the next in succession, on a certain day, while deer-stalking, went into a dispute with the Golavarapatti people, when with his sword in his left hand, he cut down a horse and its rider. From that time forward he was called "Edawangkai" or left-handed Ketchilappa Nayakar. He once overcame the then Sethupathi in a dispute, and deprived him of his state umbrellas and two state horses, and chased him and his attendants as far as Pemalli village. The eldest son of the Zemindar's second wife, Rana Sura Ketchilappa Nayakar, got into the good graces of Muthuvirappa Nayakar, received as gift, certain villages attached to Kurumalai and settled down there.

It was in the administration of the next Zemindar, Jagavira Rama Ketchila Ettappa Nayakar Aiyan, that protection was given to the Catholic priests living there. The following inscription on a stone is still in existence:—

"Year—year 865, the 19th day of the month Chitra. We Jagavira Ettappa Nayakar Avergal (make proclamation as follows): As in our father's days, twenty-five years ago, this church of God in our territory and the Matha of the ascetics of the city of Rome were preserved from harm, so also now we being resolved to do the same have visited this church and the priests and have given and set up this stone. Wherefore if any person should do any harm to this church of God or the priests, or their disciples, not only will he become a traitor to us, but let him also incur the guilt which would ensue from slaying a black cow and Brahmans on the banks of the Ganges. Thus we have ordained as long as sun and moon endure. Jagavira Ettapa Nayakar. May the Lord preserve (us)."

The 27th ruler, Jagavira Rama Venkateswara Ettappa Nayakar Aiyan was very religious and also said to be well-skilled in magic and witchcraft. The Rajah of Ramnad besieged the fort of Anamanthakudi and sought the aid of the Zemindar of Etaiyapuram, who lost no time in sending a force of 5,000 armed men. It was during this reign that the Vishnu temple at Etaiyapuram was constructed and dedicated. The Zemindar was a great patron of learning. He gave substantial rewards to Kadigai Muthu Pulavar for his *Samudra Vilasam*, and *Kumaresa Manjari*.

Muthu Jagavira Rama Cumara Ettappa Nayakar, the 31st Zemindar, was also well known for his wisdom and valour. He had a standing army of 6,000 men. He was the first to render meritorious services to the British Government by defeating the adherents of a refractory Poligar, Cataboma Nayakar of Panjalamcurichy, who defied the authorities and set at naught their measures. The then Collector, Mr. Lushington heard favorable accounts of the most opportune help of the Zemindar of Etaiyapuram who went there with a small army against Cataboma Nayakar.

In recognition of the timely help given by the Zemindar of Etaiyapuram in the defeat, pursuit, and capture of the rebel chief Cataboma Nayakar, the British Government made him a grant of the village of Sivagnanapuram. The chief was executed and one of his accomplices, Kumaraswami Nayak, his brother, was imprisoned with many others at Ramnad. A conspiracy was formed to release the latter. The conspirators successfully proceeded to the jail, overpowered the guards, entered and threw open the prison doors. This over, they proceeded to Panjalamcurichy and erected a fort well manned by a garrison of 5,000 men all ready and eager for the fight. A small army of the British fired and killed 160 men at one discharge when the remainder beat a precipitate retreat. Mr. Lushington, the Collector, who was then at Nagalapuram, wrote to the Etaiyapuram Zemindar, requesting him to make a thorough enquiry and to submit him a full report on the exact position of affairs, which he accordingly did. On receipt of the report, Mr. Lushington, with a small army proceeded to Panjalamcurichy *via* Etaiyapuram duly intimating the fact to the Zemindar in advance to make the necessary arrangements. On arriving at Etaiyapuram, Messrs. Lushington and Cassamajor consulted the Zemindar as to the course they should adopt in carrying out their object, and also demanded assistance from him in the operations against that fort. The Zemindar, as it was his wont under such circumstances, promised them all the aid in his power and requested them to supply him with fire arms and other requisites, as he and the Poligar of Panjalamcurichy were on hostile terms. The necessary arms were forthwith furnished to the Zemindar's men and three hundred additional muskets were subsequently supplied to them. Lieutenants Laughton, Lauden and Warren with three companies and some guns were sent to the protection of Etaiyapuram.

Muthu Jagavira Rama Kumara Ettappa Nayakar Aiyan died after ruling 33 years and he was widely known for his piety, generosity and other good qualities.

Jagavirarama Venkateswara Ettappa Nayakar Aiyan, who came next in succession, erected a temple dedicated to Subramanyaswami and allotted two villages yielding annually Rupees 900 for its up-keep and maintenance. He erected a choultry and sank a well at Etaiyapuram. In 1827 the Right Honorable S. Lushington, Governor of Madras, paid a visit to Etaiyapuram.

A stone *mantapam* of exquisite workmanship was erected by the Zemindar at a cost of Rupees 30,000, in honor of Calugachala Murti (a Hindu God).

A palanquin and jewels of the value of Rs. 20,000 were presented to the same idol. The lakshadwipam (one lac of lights) ceremony was performed on a very grand scale at a cost of a large sum of money. Rs. 50,000 were spent in connection with the *ashtabandanam* (the ceremony of fixing an idol) which was performed in honor of Saliwateswarar and Sri Kanthimathi of Tinnevelly. He established a choultry at a cost of Rs. 15,000, which is still in existence, and in which Brahmins and Goshais are supplied with food *gratis* every day. He built some more temples and they are all even to this day maintained by the members of his family. The excellent buildings known as Sundaravilasam, Kaliana Mahal, Subramania Vilasam, and others that grace the town of Etaiyapuram were built in his time. The two flags of honor promised to the Zemindar's father were received then. He left behind him five sons, Jagavira Rama Kumara Ettappa Nayakar Aiyan, Venkateswara Ettu Nayakar, Muthuswami Pandian and Ramaswami Pandian. The eldest of these succeeded to the estate and built a new palace in the place of the old one which he pulled down. He also erected a substantial brick fortress instead of the old mud fort. The edifice known as "Shunmugavilasam" with a golden cupola was built by him. Some roads, especially the fine and broad one leading to Naduvirpati, were constructed under his orders. Villages yielding an annual income of Rs. 2,500 were set apart for the festivals of the Siva and Vishnu temples. Villages yielding Rs. 7,600, annually were made permanent endowments for the up-keep of the temple of Subramaniaswami. The great mantapam at Kalugumalai was also erected in his time. Jewels set with precious stones of the value of Rs. 70,000 were presented to Subramaniaswami and his Tamil verses in praise of Siva, Vishnu, and Subramaniaswami bear testimony to his ripe scholarship. Two bridges, one at a cost of Rs. 6000, and another at Rs. 10,000, respectively, were built by him. The Government of Madras placed on record their high appreciation of his public spiritedness and benevolence. His bounty and munificence did not end here, for he also built a choultry at Vepalpate and endowed two villages yielding Rs. 1500, annually for its up-keep. When he died he left no heirs and hence his brother, Jagavira Rama Venkateswara Ettappa Nayakar Aiyan succeeded to the estate. He spent a large sum of money in erecting mantapams and other appendages to the Siva temple there. Notable among the additions to the palace was the Hall of Installation surmounted with five golden cupolas costing Rs. 7,000. He also died childless and therefore his brother Muthuswami Jagavira Rama Ettappa Nayakar Aiyan came to the possession of the estate. He had an interview with the then Governor of Madras, when His Excellency visited the Tinnevelly District. Swami Dikshidar, the author of Chambu Kairam, a portion of the Skunda Puranam, was publicly honored and rewarded by the Zemindar.

A silver *howdah* and a car at a cost of about 20,000 Rupees were prepared for the use of the Kalugumalai temple. He left behind him two sons, the elder of whom succeeded him.

Jagavira Rama Kumara Ettappa Nayaker Aiyan had the honor of welcoming H. R. H. the Prince of Wales, now King Edward VII, when he landed at Tuticorin in

December, 1875. The Zemindar travelled with His Royal Highness as far as Koilpati. We give the following lengthy extract relating to the visit of His Royal Highness to the Tinnevelly District :—

" At last we reached *terra firma*. The preparations were pretty; but there was really very little time to look about one. A temporary pavilion or Pandal had been erected, in which the inevitable address was delivered, and the Zemindars were presented; and when the exchange of courtesies had ended, the Prince walked to the station, where he waited till the exhausted and exhausting Margaret Northcote, had delivered her luckless freight. It is scarcely possible to exaggerate the quiet charms of the scenery along the new Railway, or the great delight of the people at the combined attractions of the first Train, and of the Prince. The whole population thronged to the road-side. The tall, erect figures, square shoulders, broad chests, narrow flanks, and straight limbs of the men, struck one almost as much as the graceful carriage and elegant forms of the women. It would be difficult to find a finer race in any part of the world. Their attitudes of wonder and joy were singularly graceful and attractive. Some expressed their feelings by placing their hands, clasped as if in prayer, before their breasts; others held their fingers to their lips, as if to suppress their cries; but as the Train passed, one and all clapped hands, as if they were of a London audience, applauding at a Theatre. A more natural, easy, and well-to-do looking people could not be found in Christendom. Plains green with sugar, rice and cotton, spread to the foot of the wooded Hills of gniess rock, which, generally conical, were sometimes worn into fantastic outline of castle-like crag, and beetling precipice. It is certainly a land, if not flowing with milk and honey, inhabited by a population of sweet and kindly disposition, whose virtues are admitted by Missionaries, and whose exceeding tractability has gained for them the praise of masters, not always given to indulge in over-laudation of any native virtues.

"The part of India, which the Missionaries call Tamil-land, is larger than Bavaria, Saxony, Wurtemburgh, and the German Dukedoms together, and contains a population of about sixteen millions of peope. The Neilgherries rising to the height of 8,000 feet, the Pulney with peaks 7,000 feet high, and their eastern offshoots, diversify the surface; and the watersheds throw off supplies for the great rivers, which become, however, for part of the year, little more than beds of sand. Coffee is planted on the lower ranges; rice in great quantities is cultivated in the plains, and sugar cultivation is extending. Indigo and different kinds of grain thrive in parts of the District, if so it may be called, and cotton is not only sufficiently abundant for the wants of the native manufacturers, but gives margin for export. The manufacture of iron, of very great excellence, the ore of which, is found in large quantities throughout is still carried on. Here we have the Salt Tax and monopoly in full force, the French at Pondicherry receiving £40,000 a year for prohibiting the manufacture within their Settlements; the revenue of the Tamil District from this objectionable source amounting to about two millions of Rupees per annum.

"At Maniachi, 18 miles from Tuticorin, a deputation of about 6,000 native Christians including a large body of clergy and catechists, and 1,000 boys and girls receiving education in Church of England schools, awaited the arrival of H. R. H. The Prince of Wales, the Rev. Dr. Caldwell, the able and learned Missionary of the Society for the Propagation of the Gospel, and the Rev. Dr. Sargent, a veteran representative of the Church Missionary Society, surrounded by a considerable staff of English clergy, stood on the platform side by side typifying the perfect unanimity with which our two great Church societies are laboring for the evangelisation of India. When H. R. H. alighted from his carriage, the Missionaries were presented to him by Mr. Robinson and Canon Duckworth. Dr. Caldwell, read an address of welcome from the Church of Tinnevelly expressing the devoted loyalty of its members and their deep sense of the special blessings they enioyed as the Christian subjects of a Christian sovereign. The progress of the Church of England Mission in this region was sketched, and it was shown how the good seed conveyed from Tanjore by Schwartz about the end of the last century and that which was sown broadcast from 1820 onwards by Rhenius, both German Missionaries in the employ of English Societies, had been nurtured by Missionaries since 1840, until the Native Christian community in Tinnevelly is the most numerous in India. Christian congregations have been formed in about 900 towns, villages, and hamlets composed exclusively of converts. The total number of Native Christians in the District was stated to be sixty thousand, who are under the charge of 54 Native clergy and 590 catechists, and teachers of various grades; and the number of communicants is 10,378. The schools are attended by about 13,000 boys and girls. It is worthy of note that the Christians in Tinnevelly contributed last year Rs. 32,483 for the support of their own church equivalent in the sacrifice it represents to eight or ten times the amount in England. At the conclusion of the address, a handsomely bound Bible and Prayer Book, in the Tamil language, and offerings of embroidery and exquisitely fine lace, the handiwork of girls attending the Tinnevelly schools were presented to His Royal Highness."

"At 12-20 P. M., the Train stopped at Koilpati, 36 miles from Tuticorin. There was a small camp and a handsome mess-tent fitted up luxuriously near the station. The tents belonged to the minor Zemindar of Etaiyapuram who was there with his kinsfolk and tenants, and the usual mighty multitude to greet the Prince. Once more we had occasion to wonder at the swarming masses and to admire the fine forms, pleasant manners and looks, and picturesque appearance of the people. There was a halt of half an hour for luncheon and, before the Prince resumed his journey, he accepted from the Zemindar some articles of trifling value as mementoes of his visit."

The Zemindar was one of those that were invited to be present at the Imperial Assemblage held at Delhi in 1876, when he had an interview with the then Viceroy and Governor-General of India, and received a gold medal from him with the following certificate :—

CERTIFICATE.

"By command of His Excellency the Viceroy and Governor-General this certificate is presented in the name of Her Most Gracious Majesty Victoria, Empress of India, to Jagavira Rama Cumara Ettappa Nayakar, Zemindar of Etaiyapuram, son of Muttusawmy Jagavira Rama Ettappa Nayakar, in recognition of his loyalty and fidelity to the British Government and charity to the poor. 1st January 1887."

He was thus enabled to travel throughout India, escorted by a Public Officer of rank, under the orders of the Madras Gvernment. He was one of the few who were invited to attend the assemblage from Southern India.

In the course of his travels to and from Delhi and other parts of India on the same occasion, under the special orders of the Government of Madras, he was escorted by a Public Officer of rank.

When famine raged most furiously in 1877-78 the Zemindar established feeding houses and thousands of people were fed *gratis*. He further extended his right hand of sympathy to his ryots by advancing them large sums of money. The following that appeared then in the proceedings of the Court of Wards will not be out of place here :—

" The interest displayed by the minor Zemindar in the management of the charities is highly creditable to him.

2. The Collector will intimate to the minor Zemindar their high appreciation of his conduct on this occasion."

We give the following remarks made by the Judge of the Subordinate Court of Tinnevelly in the decision given in favor of the Zemindar in the suit brought by his paternal uncle :—

" Here the plaintiff described the Etaiyapuram Estate as a simple Zemindari created at some time prior to 1783, (*i. e.*, during the Mahomedan period) and denied at the first hearing that it was an ancient Polliam. Consequently I cast upon 1st defendant the burden of establishing that it was a Polliam and not a mere Zemindari, which, as already observed, does not necessarily imply impartibility. Whether the estate existed as a Polliam prior to the Mahomedan rule or not, is thus the next question for consideration. The plaintiff's own exhibit A (the History of Etaiyapuram published by one Swami Dikshadar) shows that the family was founded so far back as in A.D. 803; that 36 successions intervened between the original founder and the present 1st defendant; and that during this long period of 1,000 years there was not a single instance of a partition having taken place of the estate. Throughout this book the Polligar is spoken of as a sovereign prince. It is true that this book was filed by plaintiff for the limited purpose of showing that his grandfather was not the son of his immediate predecessor; but this will not prevent the Court from reading the whole book as one document and availing itself of other informations therein contained. * * *

"For the foregoing reasons I find that the Estate of Etaiyapuram was a Principality; that from the nature of its constitution, as a sort of sovereignty, it has been all along impartible; and that the villages acquired during the time of Plaintiff's grandfather and father form accretions to it and are therefore equally impartible."

He made to the Local Board a free gift of the road leading to Calugumalai, 8 miles long, laid out and maintained at his own cost. For the completion of the bridge at Srivaikuntam across the Tambraparni he lent with the approval of the Government, Rupees 35,000 to the District Board of Tinnevelly. His tenants were greatly benefited during his time since all the irrigation works underwent thorough repairs.

Though he was liberal-minded and generous to a fault, yet he was able to effect a large saving. He built a palace on modern style at a cost of two lakhs of Rupees, and this has added much to the picturesqueness of the town. During his time education made great progress in his estate through the establishment of endowed schools.

The Zemindar acquired a wide reputation for munificence and nobility of heart, and after a brief illness he passed away in May, 1890, amidst the universal regret of his friends, relations and ryots.

The present Zemindar, Sri Rajah Jagavira Rama Venkateswara Ettappa Nayakar Bahadur was born in 1878. Till 1890, proper arrangements were made for his education, and he applied himself with industry and zeal to the acquirement of knowledge. Soon after his father's death, the Court of Wards undertook the management of the estate, and sent the young Zemindar to Madras for education. He was trained by educationists of much experience and moral worth such as Messrs. Potts, Ellison, Morrison, Payne, and Rai Bahadur K. Jagannadha Chettiar. While under the care of Mr. Morrison he travelled with him to almost all the places of importance in the Madras and Bengal presidencies, and Colombo, by land and by sea, and learnt the manners and customs prevailing in those places. Under the care of his veteran instructors he devoted himself to study and a preparation for his after life. At the same time, he did not neglect the accomplishments of a well-born Zemindar, and became a keen sportsman and a good rider.

In December 1899, the Rajah attained his majority, and the Government of Madras installed him on the *guddi* of his ancestors. The ceremony took place on a grand scale when there were present the Collector of the District and many other prominent officials. In the course of the speech made on the occasion he thanked the Government of Madras, and said:—

"It is now my pleasant duty to thank the Madras Government, the Court of Wards and the several Collectors, who were in the district since the assumption of the management by the Court of Wards, for the education they have given me and for the excellent management of my estate during my minority, and thank specially Mr. Bedford for the honor he has done me by his personally handing over the charge of the Estate to me on this occasion."

The Rajah thanked the officials of his Samasthanam, and his respective guardians in the following terms:—

"I am certainly proud to mention the name of Mr. V. Venkatroyer here who was managing the estate under the Court of Wards in the beginning; and all his good work could be seen in the whole of the estate. He was universally liked and respected for his good work and ability. He was succeeded by M. R. Ry. P. Sivarama Iyer Avergal, B.A., as manager and he has managed the estate satisfactorily; and it is in his time that an addition was made to the estate by the purchase of a large portion of Gandamanayaganoor and I thank him for all he has done towards the improvement of my estate and for the excellent manner in which he conducted my marriage festivities.

"I also thank my several guardians, Messrs. Potts, Ellison, Morrison, Payne and Rai Bahadur K. Jagannadha Chetty Garoo who have all taken such deep interest in my welfare.

"Lastly I assure you I will make it my sacred duty to manage my estate without deviating from the path of virtue and justice; and wish to avail myself of this opportunity to present this sunnud to Rai Bahadur K. Jagannadha Chetty Garoo with whose experience, I hope to give satisfaction in the management of my ancient and important Zemindari.

"Thanking you again, ladies and gentlemen, for your extreme kindness in attending this installation ceremony, I fervently pray for the speedy termination of the Transvaal troubles in favour of Great Britain and Ireland and for the long life, sound health and prosperous rule of Her Most Gracious Majesty the Queen-Empress of India."

The Rajah of Ramnad telegraphed the following message of congratulation on the occasion:—

"My heartfelt congratulations to you on your assumption of charge of your ancient and historical estate. My fervent prayers to Sree Ramanatha and to Kalugachala Shanmuga Moorthi to grant you long life and continued prosperity and to make you and your truth flourish. I have little in the way of advice except to beg you most earnestly as the son of one who was to me devoted brother to take my complete failure as a Zemindar as sufficient warning to you in your future career and to remind you of the words of Lord Ripon to the Nizam, 'look to your finance,' an advice which I disregarded but which I must beg you to bear in mind to avoid the consequences. I suffer by disregarding it. You know what great affection and regard I have for you personally and it is that that prompts me, even presses me to wire to you thus opening my heart to you. Your manager, Mr.

Sivaramier is in a way my guardian and I have fatherly regard for him. I regret his leaving you. I am performing Abhishekam and Archanai in your mame this day grandly to my Lord Sree Ramanatha and to our Divine Mother and will send you *prasadam.* Be ever loyal to our Sovereign and Her Government and use your wealth, power, and influence to benefit others, and to injure none, and above all, be devoted to the feet of Him who from Kalugachalam protects you all, and thus you will be happy now and ever."

Mr. G. S. Forbes telegraphed thus :—

"Sincere congratulations undertaking management your estates. Wish you every success and happy and prosperous year."

The Maharajah of Bobbili wired as follows :—

"Hearty congratulations on your taking charge of your estate."

The Court of Wards desired to replace Mr. Payne who was obliged to go to England on urgent private affairs by an officer who would not only be competent to instruct the young Zemindar in regard to the management of his estate but would also be a suitable person for retention after the property passed the hands of the Government of Madras. Rai Bahadur K. Jagannadha Chettiar, an officer of marked ability, unblemished reputation and long experience was specially selected for that post. He was Dewan of the estate for about 2 years and worked with much success. He lately retired on a decent pension. The present Dewan is Mr. S. T. Shunmugam Pillai, B. A., a retired Deputy

Collector of much experience. With the intelligence of the Rajah Sahib coupled with that of his able and energetic Dewan, the Samasthanam is sure to thrive and prosper.

The Rajah Sahib was under the care and tuition of competent Englishmen of great parts, and the advantages derived from his travel to various parts of the country, opened his eyes to reforms in social life, and the first item he desired to practically carry out was the opening of a Girls' School in his estate. During his father's time there was an English school teaching up to the Lower Secondary standard, and the present Rajah raised it to the grade of a High School. Etayapuram is a very large estate, where a High School was a desideratum for a long time. These measures tending towards education were carried out by him soon after he assumed charge of the estate. He has opened a model farm on scientific principles, and this in itself is sufficient to prove that he is just paving the way for higher reforms in point of cultivation. He has also established a choultry, a school, and a market at Veppalpatti.

In honor of the Coronation of King Edward VII, a meeting was held at Etaiyapuram when the Rajah made the following interesting speech :—

"GENTLEMEN,

We are assembled here, not to discuss questions connected with our private concerns, nor to express our views on party or public questions of any kind, but to perform a most solemn and sacred function of paying homage to our Most Gracious Sovereign, His Majesty, the King-Emperor Edward VII, this the most memorable day of his Coronation, in the City of London, being the capital of his world-wide dominions, on which, you all know, the Sun never sets, and further to express our sentiments of congratulation on that happy event, and of our loyalty and devotion to the British Crown of unrivalled splendour and glory.

"It is no exaggeration to say that we (Indians) are deeply indebted to the British Raj for the innumerable benefits we have been enjoying under its suzerainty, such as gigantic irrigation and water supply projects, noblest charities in the establishment of Hospitals and Chattrams, rapid advance in Education, Civilisation, Religious liberty, Art, Science, Literature, Trade and Manufacture, and various other privileges never before chronicled in the pages of the Indian History, and I do not think we can possibly repay the debt except by continuing to be ever most grateful and loyal to the Throne.

"I really wish I were, at this moment, present in London among the party of Indian visitors, there, partaking of the loyal functions they perform, and the grand and gorgeous spectacle they enjoy this day. As it is, I could but make a feeble attempt at what I thought the only best way of commemorating the event, by planting trees and topes, sinking wells, feeding and clothing the poor, and conducting a procession of the Emperor's portrait round the streets of this town and holding a Durbar like this, here. So far, I am glad to say, my attempt has been a perfect success, and I must not omit to thank all of my relations, friends, officers, and ryots, as my success is due mainly to their hearty co-operation and assistance throughout, and we all see, this afternoon, the Heaven has also accorded its sanction to our arrangements by sending, from the region of clouds, long unheard peals of thunder accompanied by rain, as if the report of our 101 guns fired is not loud enough to proclaim the happy event.

"In conclusion, I, with the full consent of the meeting, once more voice my own sentiments as well as theirs, of hearty congratulation on our Emperor's Coronation, and of our devoted loyalty to the Throne as well as the secret prayer of our heart of hearts to the Almighty God for the long life and continuously prosperous reign of His Majesty; and I propose three cheers to His Majesty the King-Emeror, and three more to Her Majesty the Queen, Empress."

The Rajah, who, in intelligence, capacity and fixed purpose, is in no way inferior to his predecessors, has undertaken what he considers as the most important duties of his exalted position, in the establishment of educational institutions, and in the introduction of scientific methods of cultivation. He is a nobleman of great promise with fine feeling, generous sympathies and an excellent and resolute character. We give the following from what Mr. Caldwell expressed in his history of the Tinnevelly District about the Etaiyapuram Samasthanam :—

"This lucid and most interesting history of Ettaiyapuram Zemindari, the most important Zemindari in Tinnevelly District may be said to form an Epoch in the literary history of the Presidency of Madras and even of Southern India, as it is not only the first connected history of an Indian Zemindari which has appeared, but is in itself a model which other Zemindars would do well to follow. The Zemindar instead of giving himself up to idleness and luxury, and leaving the best interests of his people to their fate, has set himself to imitate the public spirited and beneficent action of the best class of European nobles and not only made for himself a name and position in the foremost class of Indian local administrators, but has given his Zemindari the highest position that any Indian district of this class has yet reached. I cannot but trust that the Madras Government will take the opportunity of evincing its sense of the Zemindar's services to the State by the example he has set, and its desire that his example should be followed by others in some appropriate manner. For instance, might they not give this history, a place amongst the historical memoirs and records published by themselves, together with conferring on this model Zemindar, some title of honour, valued by natives?"

Sri Rajah A. V. Jugga Rao Garu.

Kallikote Estate Press, Rambha.

SRI RAJAH A. V. JUGGA RAO BAHADUR GARU, ZEMINDAR OF SHER MUHAMMADPURAM

(VIZAGAPATAM DISTRICT).

Of handsome person and with fascinating manners and a brilliant intellect, Sri Rajah A. V. Jugga Rao Bahadur Garu, the subject of our sketch, is a gentleman of varied attainments, and has rendered such signal service to the scientific world as cannot fail to raise him in the estimation of many a savant both of the East and the West. He has been much abroad; he has travelled through Europe and many other foreign lands, and his mind being stored with all he has seen and heard his conversation is most agreeable and instructive.

It is said that the family from which Sri Jugga Rao Garu has sprung is an ancient one, and that some of his ancestors held respectable and high posts under the Nizam of Hyderabad, prominent of them being Mr. Ankitam Sriramulu Garu, who was Dewan to the Nawab of Masulipatam. Rai Bahadur A. V. Narasinga Rao Garu, the son of Dewan Sriramulu Garu, was born in 1827. Mr. Narasinga Rao lost his father when but an infant; and so he was taken to Vizagapatam and brought up under the care of his maternal grandfather. His education was at first entrusted to Mr. Porter, and then to the Rev J. Hay, D. D., the father of modern education in Northern Circars. Mr. Narasinga Rao entered the service of the East India Company when he was young, and early rose to the position of Deputy Collector through sheer dint of energy, good character, and perseverance. He married Sri Achayamma Garu, the daughter of Mr. Goday Jugga Rao Garu.

Sri Rani Achayamma Garu, the wife of Rai Bahadur Narasinga Rao Garu, and mother of Mr. A. V. Jugga Rao Garu, comes of a very highly respectable family, the first prominent member of it being Mr. Goday Jugga Rao Garu, who came from Masulipatam to Vizagapatam as the Dubash of the then Governor-in-Council of Northern Circars, which had a special Governor in those days. Mr. Jugga Rao Garu built a temple—the only chief temple now—dedicated to Sitharamaswami, which is a living monument of his piety. He had two sons, Prakasa Rao Garu, and Narain Rao Garu. The former died heirless, but the latter was blessed with two sons, one of them being Mr. G. V. Jugga Rao Garu.

Mr. Goday Venkata Jugga Rao Garu was sent by his father to Madras for education, where he remained for some time, and made considerable progress in his studies. He had a scientific and inventive turn of mind. He built in 1874 an Observatory at Vizagapatam, and determined the latitude of the place, and also invented a Pluviometer (instrument for measuring rain). The following extracts show the position he held in the scientific world :—

MISCELLANEOUS PAPERS.

No. 1405.

From

The Meteorological Reporter to the Govt. of Bengal.

To

A. V. NURSING ROW, ESQ.,

"DABA GARDENS," VIZAGAPATAM,

Dated CALCUTTA, 22*nd August* 1870.

SIR,

I am directed to communicate to you the thanks of the Lieutenant Governor for the valuable assistance you have voluntarily rendered to this Department by forwarding your observations for collocation with those of the official observations.

I have the honor to be,

Sir,

Your most obedient servant,

(Signed) HENRY F. BLANFORD,

Meteorological Reporter to

the Govt. of Bengal.

No. 67.

From

The Meteorological Reporter to the Govt. of Bengal.

To

A. V. NURSING ROW, ESQ.,

VIZAGAPATAM,

Dated CALCUTTA, 10*th February* 1872.

SIR,

I am directed to convey to you the thanks of the Lieutenant Governor of Bengal for the valuable assistance you have rendered to this office in communicating copies of the Vizagapatam Registers.

I have the honor to be,

Sir,

Your most obedient servant,

(Signed) HENRY F. BLANFORD,

Meteorological Reporter to

the Govt. of Bengal.

No. 416.

From

The Meteorological Reporter to the Govt. of Bengal.

To

A. V. NURSING ROW, ESQ.,

VIZAGAPATTAM,

Dated CALCUTTA, 14*th August* 1874.

Sir,

I am directed to communicate to you the thanks of the Lieutenant Governor for the valuable assistance you have voluntarily rendered to this Department by forwarding your observations for collocation with those of the official observatories.

I have the honor to be,
Sir,
Your most obedient servant,
(Signed) M. G. WILLSON,
Offg. Meteorological Reporter to the Govt. of Bengal.

Extract from the Handy Book of Meteorology.

ALEX. BUCHAN.

"Since this rain gauge does not admit of very nice measurement another sort is frequently used, consisting of a receiving-vessel and a glass measure of much smaller diameter, which admits of as nice graduation as may be desired. A good specimen of this class is the gauge recommended by Mr. Symons, London, Fig, 30, in which (*b*) is the vessel which receives the rain, and (*c*) the graduated vessel which measures the amount. There being often great difficulty or trouble experienced in replacing the glass measure when it chances to get broken, the late G. V. Jugga Row, a wealthy Zemindar of Vizagapatam, proposed a gauge (Fig 31) in the form of a funnel having a diameter of 4·697 inches or a receiving area of 17·33 square inches. Now since a fluid ounce contains 1·733 cubic inches of water, it follows that for every fluid ounce collected by this gauge, the tenth of an inch of rain has fallen. The measure can of course be graduated to any degree of nicety; and it may easily be reproduced if required. It is also the cheapest rain-gauge costing only 7*s*. 6*d*. when made of copper and 4*s*. 6*d*. when made of tin. Self-registering rain gauges have been invented by Osler and Cresley; but being too expensive for general use, they need not be described."

Mr. Venkata Jugga Rao had no sons, but he had an only daughter, Sri Achayamma Garu, who was given in marriage to Mr. Narasinga Rao Garu. After the death of Mr. Goday Jugga Rao Garu, his daughter inherited his estate, and in order to manage this, Mr. Narasinga Rao resigned his post of Deputy Collector and Magistrate.

Mrs. Narasinga Rao was a lady of really fine character, elevated thoughts and noble disposition. The Government of Madras in recognition of her qualities, both of head and heart, conferred on her the personal distinction of Rani.

A cultured man himself, Mr. Narasinga Rao enlarged the observatory founded by his father-in-law by adding to it an equatorial Telescope, surmounted with a moveable dome at a cost of a lakh of Rupees, a transit instrument and a sidereal clock. He also opened a Meteorological Observatory and furnished Government daily with meteorological reports. The Government of India in recognition of his services conferred on him the title of *Rai Bahadur*. He was appointed Honorary Meteorological Reporter to the Government of India for Vizagapatam. The Government evening gun at that station having been discontinued in 1871, Mr. Narasinga Rao offered to bear the expenses of the firing which the Government of Madras allowed as a special case and this useful institution has been maintained ever since. He was elected Fellow of the Royal Astronomical Society in 1871, and of the Royal Geographical Society in 1872.

We give the following extracts we were able to collect from Government records, and also from the annual reports of A. V. Jugga Rao Observatory for the information of our readers :—

No. 465.

" *Order dated* 28*th November* 1871, *No.* 3837.

The Right Honorable the Governor in Council authorizes the firing of an evening gun at Waltair under the orders of the Officer commanding Northern District, Mr. Nursing Row paying for the powder on presentation of the necessary vouchers.

(True Extract.)

(Signed) A. C. SILVER, COL.,
Offg. Secy. to Govt.

To

THE ADJUTANT GENERAL,
Controller of Military Accounts,
Insr-Genl. of Ord. & Magazines.

(True Copy.)

(Signed) T. TAYLOR,
Hd. Clerk, Adjt. Genl's. Office.

MY DEAR MR. NURSING ROW,

I have the pleasure to forward for your perusal Proceedings of Government sanctioning the evening gun under the arrangements proposed by you. I will send the order giving effect to above from this evening by my Serjeant-Major to Vizagapatam about 4 to day. If you have any thing in the way of instruction to send to the man who regulates the clock by which the gun is fired, let me know before hand please.

Believe me,

WALTAIR, Your's sincerely,

6th Dec. 1871. (Signed) C. G. GUNNING.

Kindly return the "Proceedings of Government."

From *The Indian Magazine,* August 1887, issued by the National Indian Associstion London, in aid of Social Progress and Education in India.

REVIEW.

G. V. Juggarow's Observatory, Daba Gardens, Vizagapatm; Results of Meteorological observations, 1885. With an Introduction, containing Astronomical observations, &c., by A. V. Nursingarow, Esq., F. R. A. S., F. R. G. S., Calcutta: Thacker, Spink & Co.

Perhaps the most picturesque of all the coast districts of the Madras Presidency is Vizagapatam—the land of the Hindoo Mars, which is the meaning of the word—lying along the north-west shore of the Bay of Bengal. Here, in the chief native town of the district, lived in former days a wealthy Zemindar, G. V. Juggarow Esq., who, to the many acts of benevolence he practised among the people around him, added a great taste for scientific enquiry, especially in the subject of Meteorology; for the furtherance of which, he established there in 1841 the excellent observatory which bears his name. In the introduction to this Report of Results, Mr. Juggarow's diaries are largely quoted from, to show what had been his great desire, to provide and maintain an establishment for the accurate record of these observations, as also to communicate to the residents around "the state of my barometer or the approach of bad weather," and he enjoined upon his heirs, "in case I breathe my last before doing so, they should make the Institutions permanent at the cost of my estate." The observatory had originally been well stocked with instruments, but these becoming antiquated, others of much greater value and of recent date have been introduced by his son-in-law and successor Mr. A. V. Nursingarow, who, with the help of a number of well trained native assistants, has so carefully and regularly conducted these observations in the past, that in all subjects, such as temperature, rainfall direction and force of winds, &c., comparison is made with what had been recorded daily in sixteen previous years.

From

THE COLLECTOR'S OFFICE,

VIZIANAGRAM,

24th August, 1874.

MY DEAR SIR,

I have the pleasure to forward you the Government Order which please return after perusal on the subject of the light to be exhibited from your flag staff tower, and shall feel obliged if you will permit overseer Soobiah Nayudu to proceed with the work.

Believe me,

Yours faithfully,

(Signed) NORDMANN,

Executive Engineer.

A. V. NURSING ROW, ESQ.

No. 743.

VIZAGAPATAM COLLECTOR'S OFFICE,
5th June, 1885.

From

H. G. TURNER, ESQ.,

Ag. Collector of Vizagapatam.

To

A. V. NURSING ROW, ESQ.,

Vizagapatam.

SIR,

I have the honor to annex for your information extracts from reports to Government on the subject of the signal Tower on Dolphin's Nose.

Extracts from the Proceedings of Government, dated 13th May 1885, No. 200 Marine.

* * * Notes of Inspection by the Chief Engineer, P. W. D., 1 Circle, February—March 1885.

* * * * *

Signal Tower on Dolphin's Nose. This building is in a state of great disrepair, and has evidently been neglected for years. It is surmounted by a Flag Staff the supporting ropes of which appeared to be rotten, and the wood work might fall at any time. The present condition of the building is certainly dangerous and it should be either repaired or pulled down.

* * * * *

From J. H. Taylor, Lieut. R. N. R., Master Attendant, Madras, to the Chief Secretary to Government, dated Madras, 28th April 1885, No. 3493.

* * * * *

The signal Tower on Dolphin's Nose is private property. It is an old observatory belonging to the Nursing Row's family; it was put at our disposal for the exhibition of a lantern for the benefit of the shipping, but on the occasion of a cyclone, in October 1876, the light and portion of the house was destroyed, but the injury to the direct property was not in any way caused by the lantern or any marine interference.

* * * * *

I have the honor to be,
Sir,
Your most obedient servant,

(Signed) H. G. TURNER,
Acting Collector.

VIZAGAPATAM DISTRICT GAZETTE,
1*st May* 1886.

NOTICE.

Flag staff on Dolphin's Nose.

"It is hereby notified for the information of the public that Mr. A. V. Nursing Row has erected an expensive and durable Flagstaff on the Dolphin's Nose, and the time signals are now hoisted on it under his orders every morning between 8 and 9 o'clock to indicate time.

"The flags are hauled down at nine in the morning with great precision, and it is intended thereby to indicate the precise time of that hour not only for the information of persons whose distance from the Fort renders the report of the 9 P. M. time gun inaudible, but also to afford the Shipping in the Roads the means of finding the error of chronometers and to indicate the error of the time gun."

Rai Bahadur A. V. Narasinga Rao Garu loved, cultivated, and encouraged arts and sciences, and held men of learning in the highest esteem and confidence. He was fond of society, and his course of life was sober and regular. Lively in conversation, he kept up the dignity of his station by the most amiable and condescending behaviour.

He left Rupees 1,15,000, as an endowment for a College to be called after his wife. The College is managed by a small committee of which the Collector of the District is the Chairman, and Sri Rajah A. V. Jugga Rao Garu is the Vice-chairman. The strength of the College is 450 with Mr. P. T. Srinivasa Iyengar, M.A., L.T., a teacher of tried abilities, as Principal, who has a good staff of assistants, consisting chiefly of graduates. There is a library and reading room attached to the College for the use of the students and teachers. There is also a hostel of which the Principal is the Warden.

Sri Rajah A. V. Jugga Rao Bahadur Garu was born on the 4th February 1866, at Vizagapatam. He received his elementary education in the London Mission High School there. As for scientific education it was chiefly conducted by his father, who took a special interest in training him in astronomical and meteorological work. He made rapid progress in the study of scientific subjects by his steady application. He evinced great interest in amateur dramatic performances while young, and started an association called, "Jaganmitra Dramatic Company," whch is still in existence. He succeeded to the management of the estate in October 1898. Till then he was engaged in scientific pursuits. Besides maintaining an Astronomical Observatory opened by his father and the Celestial

Photograph Observatory started by his mother, he has expanded very much the scope of the Meteorological Observatory by providing it with all the latest instruments. He also opened a magnetical observatory which is one of the three such grand institutions in India, and is expected to be of immense use to the Government of India in the forthcoming magnetic survey of this country. The portion of the work connected with this part of the Presidency will be conducted personally by Mr. Jugga Rao Garu. He has also opened a Seismological Observatory which is a very rare institution in any country for measuring the current of earthquakes.

He has great interest in Horticulture, and has studied Botany well. He has a rare collection of standard works on Botany. Very many plants not generally found in other famous gardens of India are grown in his horticultural garden. He is a member of the International Association of Botanists.

His drawing room is an evidence of his great taste for art, and he has beautified it by some original paintings which he collected when he went to Paris.

He went to England in 1900, when he had the unique privilege of paying his respects to Her Most Gracious Majesty, the late Queen Victoria, and to the then Prince of Wales, now King Edward VII. When Mr. Jugga Rao was there, he was elected Fellow of the Royal Astronomical Society, Royal Meteorological Society, Royal Colonial Institute, and Society of Arts. While in England he visited various Observatories, and studied their working, and also visited the Agricultural Exhibition of York opened by the Prince of Wales. He stayed in Paris for a fortnight, and visited the famous Paris Exhibition, and examined all its departments. He also visited Switzerland, and the famous towns of Italy. In the various places of his visit he gathered excellent specimens of art. He has just published a very interesting diary of his travels and his opinions on most things which he saw in his tour are most lucidly given in it.

He has got a beautiful library of more than 10,000 volumes, treating on science, English literature, and Indian subjects, among them being many rare books out of print, besides the leading Cyclopædias and other books of reference.

In his mansion one can see a magnificent assemblage of all sorts of furniture, fancy things, trees and plants, forming the sublimest and at the same time the most charming scenery in all Vizagapatam. Nothing can exceed the diversified and picturesque loveliness of the landscape which is in a conspicuous part of the town. Upon an eminence stands the mansion of Mr. Jugga Rao. The grand building and the grounds occupy a large area, and the enclosure is surrounded by a wall forming a complete square. Standing high above the front storey, one could look down, with the view of a bird, upon the buildings, grounds and walls of the mansion—the sea at a short distance—and the whole circumjacent town far and wide The grand front of the mansion and the other lines of the square array of buildings that enclose the court yard are all of modern architecture. The central hall of the mansion with its lofty roof sustained by no pillars is hung with suits of armour. Passing through the entrance hall, we reach another hall, in the middle of the mansion, which contains excellent furniture and rare specimens of all kinds of novelty he was able to collect when he travelled in Europe. Suffice it to say that all the apartments are of the most splendid description, for they are all embellished with elaborate sculpture work and the furniture bear scientific evidences of their pristine richness and elegance.

In the central hall of the mansion there is a statue of Jupiter, mounted on a beautiful silver dome which was presented to Sri Goday Jugga Rao Garu, by the late Sriman Srinivasa Pillai, Dayawant Bahadur, and others with the following inscription :—

PRESENTED.

To

GODAY VENKATA JUGGA RAO, ESQ.,

On his departure from Madras.

BY

C. Srinivasa Pillai and others, his native friends at the Presidency, who fully appreciating his public spirit evinced by his exertions for the general welfare of the Hindu community, thus express their friendship, esteem and admiration inspired by his many amiable qualities and by the successful perseverance with which he has prosecuted the improvement of his mind.

MADRAS, 14*th July*, 1838.

Sri Rajah Jugga Rao Bahadur Garu has received a bronze statue of Her late Majesty Queen Victoria from England, and he is going to present it to the town of Vizagapatam. The canopy is in course of construction; as soon as it is finished, the statue will be unveiled by H. E. the Governor of Madras.

He has constructed a hospital at his own cost in a conspicuous part of the town. This has been of great help to those who require medical aid. He has erected stone posts in many places to enable the heavily laden labourer to rest his burden on for a while. A rest house in Waltair owes its existence to him.

His friends have received every proof of his natural goodness of heart as well as of his candor and prudence. He is very affable, courteous, and kind to everybody; and in almost all the circles of Vizagapatam he is spoken of well and received with great respect.

SRI RAJAH K. R. V. KRISHNA RAO BAHADUR, B. A., ZEMINDAR OF POLAVARAM

(*GODAVARI DISTRICT*).

Sri Rajah K. R. V. Krishna Rao Bahadur, B. A., Zemindar of Polavaram, who has a bold and enterprising spirit, and the most remarkable versatility of genius, is the only graduate of the aristocracy in Northern Circars. He has become a very prominent figure in Southern India, by the initiative he invariably takes in almost all public movements, and has acquired a good reputation for his untiring energy and unflagging zeal in any matter of importance that he sets his heart upon.

The family from which Sri Rajah Krishna Rao Bahadur has sprung is of great antiquity, wealth, and influence. One of the members of the family, Mr. Venkata Razu Garu, held the important and respectable post of Sheristadar in the Krishna and the Godavari Districts. He had four sons, *viz.*, Venkatarayaningar, Ramanna Garu, Pedda Subbarayaningar, and Chinna Subbarayaningar. The family being undivided, all the brothers lived together. The father, Mr. Vankata Razu Garu, out of the money he had laid by, bought a small estate in the Krishna District, and his eldest son, Venkatarayaningar, a man of much influence and tact, acquired large estates, and in course of time his fame for charity, large heartedness, and generous instincts was spread far and wide. He constructed choultries at stated intervals from Rajahmundry, his head quarters, to Benares; and it would appear that he twice distributed

Sri Rajah K. R. V. Krishna Rao Bahadur. B. A.

Kallikote Estate Press, Rambha.

his weight in gold to poor Brahmins and other poverty-stricken people of the District; and in times of famine he left the tax uncollected. After Mr. Venkatarayaningar, his widow began to manage the estate. As it was a large one, and as she had no experience, she lost every thing. A cousin of Venkatarayaningar, Jagannadha Rao, owned the present Polavaram estate, Taduvoy and Jangareddy Gudiem, and Ganapavaram estates, and also the present Gutata estate. These estates were not then so flourishing as they are now, and hence they did not pay the proprietors well. The Gutata estate passed to the hands of the Shroff of Mr. Venkatarayananingar, who was a dependant of the family. A partition took place, when Jagannadah Rao, retained to himself the present Polavaram estate and gave away Jangareddy Gudiem and Taduva estates to Pedda Subbarayaningar, and the Ganapavaram estate to Ramanna Garu. The estates of the latter two were partly sold, and partly lost to Government. Jagannadha Rao had a son, named Ramachandra Venkata Krishna Rao, who had a son, named Venkata Jagannadha Rao, and also a daughter. Venkata Jagannadha Rao died at the comparatively early age of 25, leaving behind him a young widow, Kamayamma Garu, and gave her the option of adopting a son of her own choice. She adopted her sister's son Mr. Krishna Rao, the subject of our memoir. Mr. Pedda Nagaraja Rao Garu was the great grandfather of Mr. Krishna Rao, and enjoyed the honor and privilege of being the leader of the Bar in the Provincial Court at Masulipatam. He was known to be of very high legal attainments, a great Sanskritist, and a renowned poet in Sanskrit and Telugu. He is the author of Sakuntalapraniam in Telugu, and of several commentaries on Sanskrit books.

Kamayamma Garu, the adoptive mother of Krishna Rao, was universally known for her virtue and charity. Her charity was not of the old and orthodox style, but quite in keeping with modern requirements, for she educated a number of men, most of whom are now graduates holding decent posts. What she gave away was such as to extend its usefulness to every portion of the District. Choultries and various other useful institutions established by her are the living monuments of her philanthropy and noble-mindedness.

Mr. Krishna Rao was born on the 11th November 1871, at Polavaram, in the Godavari District. While a boy of five years, he was as we have said, adopted by his mother's sister, Kamayamma Garu. He received the rudimentary portion of his education in Telugu and Sanskrit at home. The Government of Madras found that the estate was very efficiently managed by Kamayamma Garu, but the only thing that called for their remark was that the minor Zemindar was not properly educated. As she was very fond of her son it was with a pang that she sent him to Rajahmundry in 1884 for education. Soon after he joined a public school there, his intelligence shone forth with so much lustre that he gained a great reputation among the boys and teachers. With surprising rapidity he passed the Matriculation Examination in 1887. He had the capacity and inclination to learn everything that came in his way, nor was there any branch of knowledge that he despised; yet he was most inclined to mathematics and literature. In process of time when he began the study of literature and history with greater application he was looked upon as a coming man in the literary field. He joined the F. A. class of the

Rajahmundry College in 1888. In August of that year his adoptive mother died, which disturbed his studies for the remaining portion of the year. Notwithstanding the many impediments that stood in his way he joined the College the following year to resume his course of study. The adoption was just then threatened by an upstart, named Venkata Razu, who had nothing to do with the family. Unfortunately Mr. Krishna Rao's study was again disturbed, and he could not attend college as he had to contend in the suit. Owing to this cause and owing also to his protracted illness, he could not continue his studies till 1891, towards the end of which year the suit was disposed of favorably to him. He was then in a settled mind, and was in a condition to resume his collegiate course. With a mind resolved to take the degree at any cost—fortunately nothing interfered with him—he joined the F. A. class of the Madras Christian College, and passed the F. A. Examination in 1893. The year following he joined the B. A. class, and passed both the Language branches in 1896. About September of that year he was suddenly taken ill—so ill that his life was despaired of—which continued the whole of 1897. The following year he spent in recruiting his health, and in 1900 he appeared for the History branch, and came out successfully. After taking the degree he took charge of the estate, and made Cocanada his head-quarters.

Being actuated with a historical interest he lately travelled all over India. With the Science College in Poona he has been greatly impressed. This, he is of opinion, is a very useful and practical institution. Of the Ferguson College his impression is no less enthusiastic. Sarvajanic Sabha, he says, is a very well attended and patriotic institution unlike the so called institutions in Southern India that come to the notice of the people periodically, and seldom do any work to promote public utility.

He is an advocate of social reform, and as such has no objection to foreign travel. He once arranged to go to England for higher education; he purchased passage, outfit, &c., but was advised by doctors not to venture on a sea voyage as he was just then in poor health. As regards the National Congress Mr. Krishna Rao is of opinion that there should be a political agitation on constitutional and moderate basis. He admits that some of the members go out of the way, but he sympathises heart and soul with the movement. He has the highest respect for Mr. A. O. Hume, whose whole-hearted devotion to the political salvation of India, he greatly admires. He has an equal sympathy with the aims of the social conference; but he is afraid that it has not been a success as most of the resolutions passed are not carried out practically. He has a very great admiration for Veerasalingam Puntulu Garu, Rai Bahadur, as the only man who has the courage of his convictions.

In 1895 he started a society called the Andhrabhashojjeevani (society for the resuscitation of Telugu literature) of which he was the Vice-President for about two years, while the Hon. Mr. Anandacharlu was the President.

There had been a Telugu journal published in Rajahmundry by Mr. N. Subba Rao, some years ago and when that was removed to Madras to be edited by Rai Bahadur Veerasalingam Puntulu Garu, Mr. Krishna Rao started a magazine known as the *Saraswati* in 1898. He has been conducting the journal very ably by publishing ancient literature that had not been printed and also by supplying various kinds of useful information.

He paid a donation of Rupees 1,000, last year, to the "Widows' Home" started by Rai Bahadur Veerasalingam Puntulu Garu, at Madras. He has established a hospital at Polavaram, and this is very useful to all the neighbouring villages. There is a choultry at Kottapalli, near Cocanada, established by his mother, which he maintains. Every educational movement in the District finds in him a patron.

It was at his instance that a grand industrial exhibition was held last year at Cocanada, the first of its kind in the annals of the District. He helped a great deal towards the success of the District Conference and the Provincial Conference.

He is always busy with his books and journals, and suffers not a day to pass without adding something or other to his store of knowledge. He is very well informed on almost all the topics of the day. Affable and courtly in his manners he has all the accomplishments of a perfect gentleman. He is one of the best products of half a century of Western education, and the most sanguine expectations of his preceptors have been amply realised. His life has thus far justified the high promise of his early youth.

SRI RAJAH VATSAVAYA VENKATA SIMHADRI JAGAPATHI RAZU BAHADUR GARU, ZEMINDAR OF KOTHAM

(GODAVARI DISTRICT).

The surviving representative of the Peddapur Samasthanam which was once in its glory, and which is now extinct, is Sri Rajah Vatsavaya Venkata Simhadri Jagapathi Razu Bahadur Garu, who is much loved by his ryots for his generosity and kindness towards them.

From the vernacular records that are forthcoming, we understand that the ancestors of the family of the Zemindar of Kotham originally came from Northern India and settled down in Godavari, Nellore, Kristna and Vizagapatam Districts. They were divided into two sections known as Mandapathi and Vatsavayi; the former were prominent at Ongole in the Nellore District, and the latter at Peddapuram in the Godavari District. These two families acquired extensive lands not by any treacherous means but by adventure and warfare, as it was a period of chivalry, when heroism, bravery and valour were much respected and honored.

The founder of the Peddapur estate was Sri Timmarazu Bahadur Garu, who went against some of the neighbouring Mahomedan rulers, conquered them and built a fort at Peddapur. He drove away some of the Kshatryas from the village of Tirupathi as they were causing a good deal of annoyance to the surrounding Zemindars. This act won the esteem and admiration of the well-known Kings of Anga, Vanga, Kalinga and Chola. He dug a big tank at Peddapuram which is known as

"Tirupathi Raz Cheruvu." Sher Muhammad, one of the Mahammadan rulers, in recognition of the heroic spirit of Timma Razu Bahadur Garu presented him with a sword which he received holding the handle up. The custom in vogue was that the receiver of any gift should receive the thing in a suppliant posture; but the way in which Timma Razu Bahadur received the gift showed that he was in no way inferior to Sher Muhammad in point of valour.

Sri Raja Jagapathi Razu Bahadur Garu, the next in succession, erected some temples at Kattamuru, and dedicated them to Vishnu, and also built some *mantapams* and towers. He defeated a powerful Mahomedan chief, Mahomed Bêg, in battle, and took possession of such insignia, as *dhanka*, *nagar* and *nowbath*. By sheer dint of valour, he took possession of Kummuru, Bickavol, Tuni, Molleru, and Pittapur, and ruled them. He advanced towards several turbulent gangs of people in the agency tracts, brought them to subjection and made them his feudatories. He was succeeded by his son Timma Jagapathi Razu Bahadur Garu who defeated Narahari Deo in battle and captured his fort at Parlakimedi. This was done at the special request of the Maharajah of Vizianagram, Poosapathi Sitharam Razu Bahadur Garu. Timma Jagapathi Razu Bahadur Garu was very charitable, and the monuments of his charities are tanks, wells, and some other useful institutions. He died childless, and therefore his nephew Raya Jagapathi Razu Bahadur succeeded him. Nothing is known of him more than the fact of his having been very charitable to the poor. His son Timma Jagapathi Razu Bahadur Garu was a linguist, for he was well versed in a number of languages, and was also a poet. Raya Jagapathi Razu Bahadur Garu, who succeeded him, conquered all his enemies, and killed a Muhammedan ruler named Jaffer Ali near the Vindia mountains. He composed some verses in Telugu in honor of the God, Ramaswami at Bhadrachalam, and gave away Yanam, which was a sub-division of the Peddapur estate, to the French. His son Timma Jagapathi Razu Bahadur maintained a large army consisting of cavalry and infantry. He died in 1797. It was his son Raya Jagapathi Razu Bahadur Garu that obtained a permanent *sunnud* for enjoyment of lands under him from the British Government in 1802, He died in 1805 leaving behind him three widows; of whom the senior, Rani Lakshmi Narasayya Garu succeeded him. Soon after this, disputes arose as regards the succession between the Rani and Jagannadha Jagapathi Razu Bahadur Garu, the cousin of the former Rajah. The matter was referred to Government; they upheld the claims of the latter, and accordingly installed him as such. After the death of the youngest Rani in 1837, Suryanaraya Jagapathi Razu Bahadur, son of Jagannadha Jagapathi Razu Bahadur, succeeded to the estate. He was in charge of the same only for five years, during which period, owing to unforeseen difficulties such as cyclones and famine, the arrears of tax could not be paid to Government. Further the estate was encumbered with debt owing to mismanagement during the time of the Rani referred to above.

For scarcely had three years elapsed from the date of his succession, when the Collector brought the estate for sale on account of arrears. His proceedings were, however, set aside by the local Government, and they passed an order dated 4th January 1842, declining to confirm the sale on the ground that "there were strong objections to the transfer of landed property from a family who had possessed it for centuries," and remarking that "as the Collector admitted that the season had been adverse, and as it appeared from the petition of the proprietor (the father of the present petitioner) that he was desirous of entering into an adjustment of the arrears, His Lordship in Council would prefer some arrangement being made with the view of preserving the estate to the family." Then he thought that by proposing to Government to take the estate under their own management, he might effectually show them that the short collections of the Zemindari were not caused by his inability, and he accordingly made the proposal by a petition addressed to Government on the condition that it should be restored to him after the discharge of the arrears. In the meantime the Collector and the Board of Revenue had, in pursuance of the order of Government, dated 4th January 1842, recommended that as the sale of Veeravaram having been regularly completed, could not be legally set aside, the petitioner should be "allowed to retain possession of the remaining portion of the estate, consisting of six Muttas paying an annual Peishcush of Rs. 1,69,434-8-0, on the condition that the balance of arrears which, after giving credit for the purchase-money of Veeravaram, amounted to Rupees 2,55,997-10-3 should be liquidated by twenty annual instalments of Rs. 12,799-14-1, to be paid of course in addition to the current permanent *Beriz.*" Thereupon the local Government passed an order, dated 11th April 1842, directing that the property should be managed by the Collector on his account in accordance with his proposal. The Collector managed it for 5½ years, but his management did not show any better results, and the arrears were considerably augmented. At the end of that period the Collector again recommended the sale of the estate, and ultimately it was sold in auction and bought in on account of Government.

Sri Rajah Vatsavaya Venkata Simhadri Jagapathi Razu Bahadur Garu was born in 1853 at Tuni. He learnt Sanskrit and Telugu at home under able pundits, and can talk Hindustani fluently. At a comparatively early age he evinced much interest in hunting and riding, and in course of time he became an expert in both. He did not spend his time in frivolous pursuits but in careful study of vedic lore; and books treating on the ethical code of Hindus occupied a great portion of his time. He is very active and energetic, and he has developed these qualities to such an extent that he works for hours unfatigued.

The present Zemindar some years ago appealed to His Excellency the Governor in Council to restore the estate owned by his ancestors.

HIS PRAYERS WERE :—

1st. That the Government would be pleased to restore his Zemindari to him with all its profits, after deducting the annual Peishcush and the charge of management from the collections of the twenty years from 1842 to 1862.

2nd. That, if the Government did not consider that he was entitled to a remission of the whole balance due by his father, they would be pleased to restore the estate to him with all surplus funds which might now remain to its credit, on condition of his paying the balance of Rupees 2,55,997 minus such portion of it as they might think proper to remit, or of paying the whole if no remission was thought proper, or,

3rd. That if His Excellency considered that the surplus funds could not be paid, His Excellency would be pleased to restore his Zemindari to him.

The prayers of the Zemindar did not meet with a favorable response.

As soon as the Rajah Sahib took charge of the estate, he established a choultry at Tuni, where a large number of people, irrespective of caste, colour or creed are fed *gratis* every day. There are special wards for each caste. There is a separate establishment for the management of the choultry, and those who go there are highly satisfied with the treatment they receive at the hands of those in charge of it.

The Rajah Sahib lately contributed towards the Lady Dufferin Fund, Rs. 2,000, Rs. 1,000 to the Victoria Memorial Fund, and Rs. 200 to the Seshadri Memorial Fund.

Being a great Sanskritist himself, the Rajah Sahib is an admirer and encourager of Sanskrit study. Till a few years ago he had in his Samasthanam a well-known pundit ***Mahamahopadyaya*** Sriman Paravastu Venkata Rangachariar.

He maintains eight Hindu temples at the head quarters of his estate, and in the month of Karthika (December) ceremonies are performed on a grand scale at a cost of a thousand Rupees. On these days hundreds of poor people are fed.

The Rajah Sahib has excavated many channels and tanks. When famine threatened furiously in 1899-1900, he spent Rs. 10,000 at the request of Government on repairs to tanks and channels.

He has much faith in Ayurvedic medicines. He has studied medicine well and is a great doctor. He prepares excellent drugs, mixtures, &c., and gives them away free to all people. He has English, Ayurvedic and Unani medicines with him. He maintains an establishment for preparing and administering them.

He once went out hunting in one of his forests, and chased two tigers to a distance of 12 miles, and ultimately shot them dead. He has killed a number of tigers and cheetahs. He would ride on horse back wherever possible, and go walking long distances at a stretch while on hunting excursions. He is undoubtedly a keen sportsman. He has trained a number of animals to peform different kinds of feats. Horses of the best mettle, goats and sheep of excellent breed he has in his menagerie, and their performances in the ring are simply wonderful. Those animals have been trained under the immediate supervision of the Rajah Sahib and they are all kept in good order.

He has a press of his own with a large establishment for the purpose of printing rare medical books. All the proofs pass through his hands; he does not grudge the trouble of going through them carefully.

The Rajah Sahib is extremely kind to his ryots. He advances them money for purposes of cultivation. He makes large remissions during famine times, and hence they do not emigrate to other places in times of difficulty. Though he is said to be orthodox his views are very liberal. He is very loyal to the British Government, and is a friend of every one of the Collectors of the District. He is held in the highest estimation by his ryots, and is very popular with the general public.

SRI RAJAH VENKATA RANGIAH APPA RAO BAHADUR, ZEMINDAR OF KAPILESWAR MUTTA, NUZVID

(*KRISHNA DISTRICT*).

The Nuzvid Zemindari family is perhaps the oldest of the families of Zemindars in the Krishna District, and in olden days some of the members distinguished themselves in battle, attained great successes in the field and thus rose to prominence. The present representative Sri Rajah Venkata Rangiah Appa Rao Bahadur, a member of the Nuzvid family, and the Zemindar of Kapileswar Muttah, has had the benefit of Western education, and having travelled to most of the important places in India, accompanied by his tutors while he was under the management of the Court of Wards some years ago, has been able to manage his estate without any difficulty.

The first member of the family of whom anything is known was Meka Basavanna who hailed from the south, and established himself on the left bank of the river Krishna some two hundred years ago. It is said that he built a small fort near Gollapalli, which was then a debatable land and a battle field for the armies of the Orissa Rajahs, of the King of Vijianagar, and of the Nawab of Golconda. The fort must have been an insignificant one, or else it would have drawn the attention of those powerful chiefs. In 1667, Appanna, generally known as Vijaya or "victorious" added much to his ancestral estate, and received from the Nawab of Golconda the titles of *Thahavar va zalalat* and *dastugaha* with some insignia of royalty. He was further given the titles of

Sri Rajah Venkata Rangiah Appa Rao Bahadur.

Kallikote Estate Press, Rambha.

Rajah, Bahadur, and Appa Rao, which have been used by all the succeeding members of the family. The fort now at Nuzvid owes its existence to Rajah Vijaya Appa Rao Bahadur. There is a legend to the effect that on a certain day as he was going on a hunting excurtion he came to a field of gingelly oil seed, where a goat was defending itself most furiously against the attacks of a wolf. This the Rajah considered to be a good omen inasmuch as a feeble animal successfully resisted a mighty one, and on the spot he built his fort; and hence Nuzvid is derived from *Nuvid chetta vidu* (the place of the oil seed plant).

Sri Rajah Narasimha Appa Rao Bahadur, the next prominent member of the family, received the title of *Teen hazar mansubdar* which meant that he held his estates on the feudal tenure of leading three thousand men to the standard of his suzerain or lord. He was a very successful and popular ruler, and many poems were composed in his honor by the prominent poets of those times. The Rajah died childless, and hence the estates passed to a distant relation named Appanna, and on his death, to Ramachandra, also called Narasimha Appa Rao. It was in the time of Ramachandra that Asaf Jah, Subadar of the Dekhan, went to the Krishna District to bring it under the central authority. Ramachandra set himself resolutely to the task of defying the authority of the Subadar, and stood a siege which lasted for three months in the Nuzvid fort, but fell a victim to the sword of Rustum Ali Khan, who kept the estates for twelve years; but his successors were not able to manage them, and so they arranged to rent them out. Under the influence of two members of the Kamadana family who were dependants on the Rajahs of Nuzvid, one Venkatadri a descendant of the Nuzvid family, took the eighteen parganas of his ancestor for rent. The Kamadana people exerted their influence with the Nawab of Hyderabad and got a permanent sunnud for those parganas in the name of Venkatadri, but before they returned, Venkatadri had died. However, his brother Jagannadha received the sunnud. The new Zemindar in a short time turned against his benefactors, and in the struggle that ensued they made him prisoner. Before setting him free they wrung out a promise from him to give them the management of the Nidadavole and Pentapad parganas; but he failed to fulfil his promise as he tried to expel them from his jurisdiction when he had regained his liberty. They used their influence again with the Nizam of Hyderabad and succeeded in obtaining a sunnud for the whole of the Nuzvid estates. When this fact reached the ears of Appa Rao he was in a fix, and scarcely had the Kamadana people arrived from Hyderabad, when he offered them the whole of the Charmahal estate on condition that they got the sunnud cancelled. This they did, but he proved false to his promise. By this time the French had established themselves at Masulipatam and were very influential in the Dekhan. They had a fort at Divi within the jurisdiction of the Zemindar. The Kamadana people made known their grievances to the French and sought their help. They wanted Appa Rao to come to terms, but he would not do so; the consequence was that a battle took place, in which he was made prisoner. He died in the prison. Thereupon the Kamadana people exerted their influence with the French, and got one Venkatadri, a lineal descendant of the family, to succeed Appa Rao. Venkatadri obtained Amaldari and Zemindari sunnuds through Hasan Ali Khan. Venkatadri Appa Rao, in token of his gratitude to his benefactors, the Kamadana people, gave away the Charmahal estate. Narasimha Appa Rao, the next in succession, managed the state badly and the tax due by him to Government fell into arrears, and as he failed to pay though repeatedly demanded, the authorities were constrained to send a small army to take possession of the estate. He borrowed money from Government officials and met the demand. As he had not paid the money borrowed from them, they brought their claims against him. He first appealed to the Governor-in-Council at Madras, and then to the Court of Directors in London. The latter ordered a strict enquiry to be made. While matters stood thus, Narasimha Appa Rao, assumed an attitude of defiance, and the result was that a small army of the British was sent against him. He made his escape to the Nizam's territory, and when an extradition for his arrest was obtained, he appeared before the Chief in Council and offered to pay his arrears if his rebellion was condoned and his estates were restored. His requests met with a favorable response, but he failed to pay his arrears, and Government were obliged to send a small army to take possession of the estate. In the severe fight that ensued, Narasimha Appa Rao escaped in disguise, and his opponents levelled the ramparts to the ground. The Government issued a proclamation to tho effect that they had removed Rajah Narasimha Appa Rao from the Zemindari, and that his elder son Rajah Venkata Narasimha Appa Rao was recognised Zemindar. The father took refuge in the jungles of Bhadrachalam and caused much annoyance to the Company's officers by burning villages, plundering treasure and killing and mutilating any who resisted. The Company's officers effected a compromise with him in 1785 and permitted him to reside with his son at Nuzvid. The father and his two wives were instrumental in fomenting these disturbances, and after his death Nuzvid became quieted down.

Ramachandra Appa Rao, one of the sons of the former Zemindar, and also one of his widows tried to follow in his wake in annoying the Company's officers, and Government took the management of the estate and granted the claimants allowances. In 1880, the authorities restored the Zemindari by issuing sunnuds to Venkata Narasimha Rao for the Nidadavole parganas and to Ramachandra Appa Rao for six parganas, and as the youngest brother of these two was yet a minor he received nothing. All arrears due to Government were relinquished, and so they were placed in charge of the estates with clear balance sheets. After the death of Ramachandra Appa Rao and Venkata Narasimha Appa Rao, the management of the estates came under the Court of Wards. Rajah Sobhanadri Appa Rao, the son of Ramachandra Appa Rao, took possession of the estate in 1831. He had in his treasury fourteen lakhs of Rupees, the accumulations of his long minority. His extravagance dissipated this hoard and in a short time he became burdened with a debt of six lakhs of Rupees. Rajah Narayya Appa Rao, the son of Rajah Sobhanadri Appa Rao, was a very enlightened Zemindar. In his time, the town of Nuzvid was cleansed, new roads were made through it, and lamp posts were erected, all at his cost. He died in 1877, leaving three minor sons; the eldest of them was recognised Zemindar, and the estates were taken under the management of the Court of Wards.

The late Rajah Sobhanadri Appa Rao, who died in 1868, left six sons. The fourth son, Rajah Venkata

Narasimha Appa Rao, presented a petition to Government, praying that the Zemindari might be divided, which petition was rejected. He then commenced a suit against his five brothers to recover a share of the estate and also the personal property left by his father. The case was decided by the District Judge of Krishna, and an appeal was preferred to the High Court of Madras against the decision of the Lower Court, and ultimately the Privy Council decided that the Nuzvid estates became a new Zemindari not feudal in its tenure or impartible in its nature, and therefore the succession to them must be regulated by the ordinary Hindu Law.

In consequence of the said decision the five surviving sons of Raja Sobhanadri became entitled to one-sixth of the estates with arrears of mesne profits, which arrears the minor sons of their eldest brother could not possibly pay out of their sixth share. The District Judge, in 1880, issued an injunction to the Collector to divide the estate and the Collector anxious to avert the ruin of the three minors, endeavoured to persuade the successful litigant to agree to some compromise. The uncle of the minors would listen to no argument. To arrange a division among claimants of this nature was a troublesome business, but in 1881 it was accomplished by the Collector who effected a compromise under which the minors retained one-sixth of the estates and a sum of money in hand. The remainder of the estates and of the money at credit of the minors was divided among the five uncles in accordance with the decision of the Privy Council.

Sri Raja Venkatadri Apparow Bahadur Garu went to Hyderabad with his elder brother Sri Raja Jagannadha Appa Row Bahadur to recover the estate of

Joojjooroo which was taken possession of by the Government of His Highness the Nizam of Hyderabad from the Kalavakollu family, of which his mother's sister was a member. He stayed about three years in Hyderabad with his brother. As His Highness was then a minor, Sir Salar Jung the Prime Minister was ruling the country on behalf of the Nizam.

Unfortunately at the end of three years, Raja Jagannadha Apparow died of malarious fever before he attained his object. When the sad news reached Nuzvid, the eldest of the brothers, Raja Narayya Appa Row went to Hyderabad leaving behind his aggrieved father who was prepared to start. He reached Hyderabad in time and soothed his other brother. He paid his respects to Sir Salar Jung who told him that he had already requested his brother to return as the settlement was difficult, but that he had not done so. Then both the brothers returned to their place. A year after, Raja Sobhanadri Appa Row died of dysentery. Then Raja Narayya Apparow, the eldest of the brothers, succeeded to the Zemindari. He gave his brother Raja Venkatadri Appa Row the charge of *Kamatams* and *Bhutadi* accounts. He performed his duty so well that he became very popular and he was consulted by his brother on important matters. After some years differences arose between the brothers. Then a suit was preferred by the Zemindar in conjunction with two other brothers, Raja Simhadri Appa Row and Rajah Venkataramayya Appa Row. Several attempts were made by Government officials and private men to effect a compromise, but the Zemindar was stubborn. He was not willing even when the brothers requested him to give them all Nunna Parganna or Rs. 1000, allowance per mensem. He agreed to give Rs. 500 each per mensem. Therefore the compromise was not effected, and the suit was continued with rigor chiefly by Raja Venkatadri Appa Row. He died before the matter was settled.

Sri Rajah Venkatadri Appa Rao Bahadur was first taught Persian under the supervision of his father. He became a great scholar in that language and also in Telugu. He was a poet and his compositions bear testimony to his ripe scholarship. He married the only daughter of Sri Malrazu Kondala Rao Garu, pensioned Zemindar of Narasaraopet. The result of this union is Sri Rajah Venkata Rangiah Appa Rao Bahadur Garu, who bears the name of this sketch.

Sri Rajah Venkata Rangiah Appa Rao Bahadur lost his father while he was three years old. The management of the estate was entrusted to his paternal uncle, Sri Rajah Simhadri Appa Rao Bahadur. Sri Rani Venkata Rama Lakshmi Kanakamma Rao Bahadur, the widow of the late Raja Venkatadri Appa Rao Bahadur, being dissatisfied with the management of Sri Rajah Simhadri Appa Rao Bahadur, took everything into her hands. She went with her son and also with a number of her relations to many places of pilgrimage in India. She was in charge of the estate only for a year, when the Court of Wards took its management under them, and sent the minor Zemindar first to Masulipatam, and then to Madras for education. At the latter place, he joined the Pacheappa's College, and read up to the Matriculation standard, during which period he was under the guardianship of Mr. R. U. Potts. The Zemindar was taken on tour to almost all the places of importance in India and

Ceylon, and thus his powers of observation were considerably improved. As a student his conduct was exemplary both towards his tutors and his classmates. We quote here his views on travel: "Every man, in my opinion, should, as far as his means and circumstances allow him travel over the world; for those who stick fast to their homes are like the frog in the fable, which deems that its abode—the bottom of the well—is the entire world, for it never comes out of it. My dear fellow countrymen, you ought to travel at least in India, for you are fortunate enough to be born in this country, which is the embodiment of all the characteristic features of the whole world. In India you can see the luxuriant foliage and beautiful animals of the Torrid Zone. In India you can also see the snows of the Frigid Zone, the picturesque mountain sceneries, the large and grand river basins, the beautiful waterfalls, and the best specimens of architecture in the world. You can meet with people of almost all the nations speaking different languages."

The Rajah Sahib appreciates highly all the good that the Court of Wards have done him and has specially thanked them for their giving him an opportunity to visit the various sacred places in India.

As soon as Sri Rajah Venkata Rangiah Appa Rao Bahadur attained his majority, he was put in charge of his Estate. As he had received a good education under Mr. Potts, he experienced no difficulty in following the lines already chalked out by Government for his guidance.

He is a father of six children, two sons and four daughters. The elder of the former, Sri Rajah Parthasaradhi Appa Rao Bahadur has been adopted by his paternal uncle, the Zemindar of the Vuyyur Estate.

He has not interfered with the charitable institutions maintained and established by his father, but has made them more permanent and useful. He is very religious, but not narrow-minded. He has been managing the estate very carefully with the assistance of a suitable staff of officials. He does not love show, but is very simple, courteous and polite. He is very kind to his ryots, and the public of the Krishna District speak very highly of his noble behaviour and gentlemanly qualities.

SRI RAJAH MRITUNJAYA NISHANKA BAHADUR GARU, ZEMINDAR OF SANGAM VALASA

(VIZAGAPATAM DISTRICT.)

One of the oldest of the living representatives of the aristocracy of Southern India bearing a good name for sagacity and nobility, is Sri Rajah Mritunjaya Nishanka Bahadur Garu, Zemindar of Sangam Valasa. He is a nobleman of varied attainments and great experience, and though well-stricken in years is to-day in the best of health and spirits, and still keeps up his studious habits. It is therefore with pleasure that we have assigned a place in this book to his biography.

The family from which the Raja Sahib has sprung, is a very ancient one, the progenitor of which was one Damodar of the lunar race, who lived in the vicinity of Nandapur, having arrived there from Northern India. By sheer dint of energy and valour he was able to obtain possession of lands near Nandapur and ultimately constituted himself king of that place. Whenever he went against his enemies, he stopped at a place called *Sangrama Veerathi* (Sangrama, meaning battle, and Veerathi, residence); this in Telugu is known as Sangam Valasa. In his line of descent there was born a king named Prataparudra, who won various territories putting down the kings of those places, and who thereby improved his own estate. He acted with such valour as to deserve the name of Prataparudra. The next prominent member of the family was Ramachandra, who was a friend of the king of Nandapur, which was not far away from his place. At that time the king of Nandapur owing to disturbances caused to him by his enemies

Sri Rajah Mritunjaya Nishanka Bahadur.

kallikote Estate Press, Rambha.

implored the aid of Ramachandar, who, in compliance with the request, defeated his enemies. For this act of valour, the king of Nandapur conferred on Ramachandar, the title of *Nishanka* (fearless), which has become hereditary. The latter had a son named, Nandanna Nishanka, who was an ornament to the family as he was well-known for his generosity. The agraharams, tanks, wells, &c., established by him yet bear his name. He had two sons, Jagannadha Nishanka and Karranna Nishanka. The elder established many useful institutions for the use of the public, and was extremely kind to all. He had nine sons, and the eldest of them, Siyyandora Nishanka, who was placed at the head of the administration followed the footsteps of his father, and thus acquired a good reputation for his noble behaviour and honesty of purpose. He had two sons, Jiyyondora Nishanka and Pàtra Nishanka; the former succeeded to the estate.

During the time of Jiyyondora Nishanka, the king of Vijianagram established his power over Jeypore, when the brother of the king of the latter place with great anger left Jeypore and settled down at Narayanapatnam, and from that place sought the assistance of Jiyyondora Nishanka, who had made him king of Narayanapatnam. Jiyyondora Nishanka had two sons, the elder Peddanna Nishanka, who succeeded the father, ruled the estate well. At this stage, the king of Pithamanipur, whose head turned on account of his great powers, fell upon, Sangam Valasa, when Peddanna Nishanka with a large army went against his enemy, and chased him as far as Belgaum. He had three sons, Thammandora Nishanka, Venkata Nishanka and Veeranna Nishanka. They lost their father when they were all young, and the eldest went away on pilgrimage; hence Venkata Nishanka was placed on the *musnud* by the British Government as he was very helpful to them when they established their power over Northern Circars. Venkata Nishanka ruled the estate for a long time. He had two sons, Peddanna Nishanka and Karranna Nishanka; the elder succeeded to the estate. His life was rendered miserable owing to family dissensions, and he therefore applied to the Rajah of Bobbili to interfere in his behalf and to effect a compromise. When Karranna Nishanka went to Bobbili on this mission, the Rajah of the latter place treated the former with great condescension, and offered him a palace to live in. There, his son, Sri Rajah Mritinjaya Nishanka Bahadur Garu, was born in April 1828, a posthumous child. As he was born at Bobbili, the Rajah of that place conceived a great liking for him and treated him as a child of his own. The British Government interfered, and took the management of the estate under them.

Sri Rajah Nishanka Bahadur Garu, when he was young, was sent to Vizagapatam, under the guardianship of his maternal uncle, Sri Medini Rao Narasimha Razu Garu. Efficient tutors to teach him different languages were appointed under the orders of Government. He was very studious and intelligent, and therefore without much effort learnt many languages. He did not waste a single moment but made the best use of his time in the acquirement of knowledge. He learnt the Vedas, and other branches of philosophical Hinduism under a great preceptor, Mahamahopadyaya Srimath Paravasthu Venkata Rangachariar. In 1847, Sri Rajah Nishanka Bahadur Garu was installed on the guddi of his ancestors, when there was much rejoicing all over the estate. His maternal uncle built a neat town, near Sangam Valasa, on account of the salubriousness of its climate, and called it Mritunjayanagar, which has since become the seat of the Zemindari, where a nice palace is built with all the modern appliances.

It is creditable to Sri Rajah Mritinjaya Nishanka Bahadur Garu that he is the only Zemindar in Northern Circars, who possesses a knowledge of many arts and sciences. He has studied medicine well, and has cured many hard cases by administering the medicines prepared by him. His knowledge of astronomy is of a high order, and he is an expert in examining diamonds. It is an acknowledged fact that he is a great architect, and a renowned artist. His musical talent is admired by all. That he is a highly accomplished Telugu scholar has been proved beyond doubt by his well-known commentaries on the following three of the works of Kalidasa :—Abhignyana Sakunthala, Vikramôrvasiya and Malavikagni Mitra. His book of morals, known as Nithi Sastra Sangraham, has become a popular one, and is highly spoken of by the educated classes. He has also published the following original works in Telugu :—Sri Sambha Sathakam, Gowree Vivaham, Raja Sekhara Vilasam, Sri Suryanarayana Charitham, Dasavathara Natakam and Parijatham. He is also the author of a book which contains a Code of Laws as a help to Zemindars.

In 1877, the Rajah Sahib convened a large meeting and addressed those present on the proclamation of the late Queen Victoria as the Empress of India. He composed some verses in praise of Her Majesty and presented them to her. On the occasion of the Diamond Jubilee of Her Majesty the late Empress of India, he was the recipient of a certificate of honour as a recognition of his ripe scholarship, and of the able management of his estate. Last year, on the occasion of the Coronation of His Maiesty King Edward VII, the Rajah Sahib got up a large meeting at Sangam Valasa, and made a grand speech expatiating on the benefits derived from British rule in general, and on the virtues of the King in particular.

To the Rajah Sahib were born seven sons; the last four of them died while young. His eldest son, Sri Rajah Chandrasekhara Nishanka Bahadur, who was an educated prince, died some years ago leaving a son, Sri Rajah Viswesa Nishanka Bahadur. The Rajah Sahib's second son has also sons and grandsons.

His Majesty King Edward VII, while President of the Royal Asiatic Society, expressed himself highly pleased with the commentaries of the Rajah Sahib on the works of Kalidasa and appointed him a member of that body.

The Rajah Sahib has been in charge of the estate for the last 56 years, and his rule, we think has been the longest amongst the Zemindars of Northern Circars. At the end of his 50th year's rule, a jubilee was celebrated at Sangam Valasa. On that most auspicious occasion his subjects prayed for his long life and prosperity, while his brother Zemindars and friends offered their congratulations.

He has saved from ruin the temple dedicated to Visweswara Swami in Sangam Valasa. He has presented valuable jewels to many temples. He is very pious, and therefore generally spends his time in the company of Pundits. He is very charitable to the poor, and is greatly popular throughout the district.

The Rajah Sahib is full of honours and years, and his counsel on matters of importance is highly valued by the educated public of the Vizagapatam District. His versatile genius, his noble behaviour, his vast and varied experiences and many other virtues that he possesses entitle him to the first place amongst the Zemindars of the District.

SRI RAJAH RAO RAMAYAMMA RAO BAHADUR GARU, ZEMINDARNI OF THE GOLLAPROLU MUTTAH

(GODAVARI DISTRICT).

In the Madras Presidency there are some rich landed estates managed most carefully by Zemindarnis, free from all encumbrances. This in itself is sufficient to prove that Southern India, more especially the Madras Presidency, is not devoid of women who can manage large estates, and to show to the outside world that their intelligence and statesmanlike qualities are not inferior to those of women in other parts of India. The Zemindarni of the Gollaprolu Muttah has been managing the estate since the demise of her husband with much benefit to the muttah and credit to herself.

Sri Rajah Rao Ramayamma Rao Bahadur Garu is the widow of the late Sri Rajah Venkata Rao Bahadur Garu, the third brother of the late Rajah of Pittapur, Sri Rajah Venkata Mahipathi Gangadhara Rama Rao Bahadur Garu, and the daughter of Sri Venkayya Garu of the well-known Chelikani family. She married Sri Rajah Venkata Rao Bahadur Garu in 1865.

Since the establishment of the Pittapur estate, it has been a custom to make the senior member its ruler. By virtue of this custom, the then senior member, Sri Rajah Venkata Mahipathi Gangadhar Rama Rao Bahadur assumed charge of the estate, and was pleased to give away the Gollaprolu muttah to his brother, Sri Rajah Venkata Rao Bahadur Garu, instead of the usual allowance. As the latter had no issues hy his wife, he married another, Venkayyamma Garu, the daughter of the Zemindar of Thangalamudi. The Rajah was cut off in the prime of life after a brief illness. The estate was then registered in the names of both the widows, the income being divided between them. Venkayyamma Garu died in 1889. In 1886, Ramayamma Garu adopted her sister's son, which adoption the Rajah of Pittapur objected to and brought a suit to cancel. The case was disposed of in favor of the plaintiff. This over, the Rajah brought another suit for the share of the deceased Venkayyamma Garu in the estate. The suit was dismissed, and the whole of the estate was registered in the name of Ramayamma Garu.

The water supply to the village of Gollaprolu at a cost of Rupees 4500 owes its existence to her generosity. She has built a choultry which is valued at Rupees 2000. She contributes Rs. 500 annually towards the expenses of the festival of Sitharamaswami. She is a Vaishnavite by birth and by profession, but she is not a conservative in religion. She admits the tenets and principles of the various branches of Hinduism as she is of opinion that they, one and all, tend towards the same goal—Mukthi (freedom from bondage). In proof of this she has built a temple for the use of the Saivites at a cost of Rupees 2000, with an endowment of lands for its upkeep. Some years ago she gave away large pieces of land to the poor people as sites to build houses on. Four hundred households are indebted to her for this piece of charity.

There is a village called by her name near Gollaprolu. She has established two water sheds, one near the Railway station, and the other in the town of Gollaprolu. She lately purchased lands and presented them to some of her most faithful servants. Two students preparing for University examinations receive monthly stipends from her. Many other students also receive help from her occasionally. She subscribes liberally to the Veda Pata Sala at Cocanada. On the Vijaya Dasami day she feeds a large number of people, and gives presents to all her servants. She has celebrated at her cost many marriages of poor people. The children of her deceased servants who are incapable of maintaining themselves are protected by this benevolent lady. Many of her relations who are poor are liberally helped by her, and some of them live with her.

She manages her estate in a most business-like manner. She is helped by a Dewan and a good staff of officials. She hears the grievances of her ryots through her Dewan and affords them speedy redress. She is very affable, courteous and kind to every body.

SRI MANYAM MAHA LAKSHMAMMA GARU, ZEMINDARNI OF THE GUTALAH MUTTAH

(*GODAVARI DISTRICT*).

The only prominent family of the Vaisya community amongst the landed aristocracy is the Manyam family, and the present representative thereof is Sri Manyam Maha-Lakshmamma Garu, Zemindarni of the Gutalah Muttah, who bears a good name, and an exemplary character.

The first member of the family to which the Zemindarni has the honor to belong was Manyam Kanakayya who flourished at Cocanada in 1790 as a negotiation merchant. He went to Yanam, started business and succeeded very well. He had five sons, Venkata Narasayya, Sathialingam, Reddiah, Venkata Rathnam and Prakasa Rayadu. Of these, Sathialingam who rose to prominence bought the Gutalah estate, which was originally in the possession of Mangapathi Deo, Maharajah of Polavaram. In 1812 the whole of the Polavaram estate was put to public auction, when Rajah Appa Rao of Nuzvid purchased it. In 1827 Sathialingam bought the same from Rajah Appa Rao for 230,000 Rupees. Till 1850 the former managed the estate, but after his death, his son, Kanakayya, and his brother, Venkatarathnam took the management into their hands. Venkatarathnam had four sons, Kanakayya, Venkatasubba Row, Seethia and Rajah Jee. In 1860 Venkatarathnam died; then the first two became joint Zemindars. As all the brothers died one after another, Kanakayya was in sole charge of the estate for about ten years. He had a son, Chinna Kanakayya, who knew English, French and Sanskrit. He built the present mansion at Yanam. He purchased from the French extensive lands of the value of a lakh of Rupees. He was highly respected by the French Government for his scholarship, liberality, and noble behaviour. He established and maintained a choultry at Yanam and another at Gutalah to feed people *gratis* irrespective of caste, colour, or creed.

Sri Maha Lakshmamma Garu is the daughter of Seetharala Sathialingam Garu, who was a merchant of Vizagapatam, and who died eight years ago. He was known for his charities in the Godavari and Vizagapatam Districts. Sri Manyam Maha Lakshmamma Garu was born in 1856, and was married to Chinna Kanakayya Garu in 1865. The happiness of their married life continued for eight years, after which period, the cruel hand of death snatched away Kanakayya. Since then Maha Lakshmamma has been managing the estate. She has acquired a great reputation for her liberality. She lately gave away *inam* lands to some poor people. Some years ago when famine raged furiously she made a remission of more than 10,000 Rupees in the tax due from her ryots She has built two temples, and has restored three ruined ones. Some years ago she went on a pilgrimage to Jagannath, where she gave away large sums of money to the poor. She feeds many people *gratis* every day in her choultry at Yanam. She contributes very liberally towards all movements started by the French Government.

When the estate was purchased by Sathialingam Garu from Rajah Appa Rao of Nuzvid, the latter sent the insignia such as *danka*, *nagar* and *chopdar* sticks, which were subsequently recognised by the British

Government. The French Government in recognition of the nobility of Sathialingam Garu, granted him permission for the beating of *nagar* in his mansion as a mark of respect.

The present Zemindarni sets out on tour whenever she finds it convenient to do so, and hears the complaints and grievances of her ryots. During the time of her former manager, owing to mismanagement, the estate was encumbered with debt, but everything has been set right after the present manager joined the staff of the Zemindarni's establishment. He has been a manager for the last fifteen years, during which period he has shown a large saving, and has thus saved the estate from decay and ruin. He is spoken of very highly by the French Governor, and also by the Judge of Yanam.

The Zemindarni is very kind to the poor of all classes, and many people depend on her bounty. Her charities are all of the advanced type and she is admired for her virtues, both as a woman and a Zemindarni.